# Breaking the
# SALT Habit

## Low Sodium Recipes Made Easy!
### written by ERIK WILLIAMS

# Breaking the
# SALT Habit

## Low Sodium Recipes Made Easy!
### written by ERIK WILLIAMS

# Breaking the **SALT** Habit!

ISBN: 978-0-615-57270-3

First Edition

Visit our web site:

**breakingthesalthabit.com**

Or email us at:

**breakingthesalthabit@gmail.com**

# an
# acknowledgement

I would like to take a moment to acknowledge all the people who have helped me with this book. Thank you to my wife Mindy, for sampling my recipes (the good and the bad). I'm indebted to my sister Kelly for her time with the design and layout of this book.

Thank you to my sister Melanie, a dietician, who looked over every recipe to ensure the proper nutritional requirements were met. I am very grateful to all of my family and friends who encouraged and supported me throughout the process of my surgery and the writing of this book. I could not have made it this far without them. And most of all, I am thankful to my donor and God for giving me this second chance at life.

# about
# organ donation

I would also like to take this opportunity to discuss the importance of organ donation. No one expects or knows when they will die, but you could find some good in a bad situation. There are currently over 111,000 people nationally who are waiting on a life saving transplant, and sadly, there are just not enough organs to go around. Unfortunately, **an average of 18 people a day die waiting.**

I have a second chance at life because of my heart transplant. If someone had not generously chosen to be a donor, I would not be alive today. I want to help others understand why the need for organ donation is so great. The fact that one organ donor can save lives of up to 8 people and one tissue donor can save/enhance the lives of up to 75 people says a lot.

On average, 144 people are added to the nation's transplant waiting list every day - one every 10 minutes. Please consider making your wishes known and register to be an organ donor at your BMV or at one of the websites listed below. While on these websites, please read the information to learn exactly what the donation process is and to learn there are a lot of myths and misunderstandings about being an organ donor. If you are still not convinced to sign up to be a donor, ask yourself this, would you take an organ from someone else to save your life or a family member's life?

**www.donatelife.net**
**www.unos.org**

**Would you take an organ** from someone else **to save your life** or a family member's life?

# table of contents

## on the side                                      **95**

# a little
# background

Growing up, I never thought of myself as different from any of my friends. In grade school, I was able to play the same sports and do everything physically that anyone else could do. In high school, I was a little more limited since my doctors did not want me to do the running and weight-lifting required to play in high school, but I always found ways to fit in.

I had those limitations because I was born with a congenital heart defect called transposition of the great arteries. This means that my pulmonary and aortic arteries were switched, causing the heart to pump blood the wrong way through my heart. As a result, I had to have two surgeries as a young child: closed-heart surgery when I was a day old and open-heart surgery when I was 2-years-old.

Doctors performed a "Mustard Procedure" to correct my heart problem as much as possible. That surgery created a baffle in the atria to restore the circulation and reversed the blood flow through the heart, making the right side the main pumping chamber. Through the years, the right side of my heart started to give out, which typically happens to children who have had the "Mustard Procedure" when they reach their 30's or 40's. Like most people who have undergone the procedure, I developed congestive heart failure and required a heart transplant to continue living.

In November 2006, I received news that I would require a transplant, but I did not know when this would happen. By following my doctor's advice to restrict my sodium intake to 2000 mg or less a day and taking my medications, I was able to extend the life of my heart another four years. During that time, I realized exactly how sodium intake affects the heart. The more I stuck with the diet, the better I felt and the more I was able to do physically. This gave me a huge head start for life with my new heart.

On May 26, 2010, at age 32, I was fortunate enough to receive a heart transplant. Learning how to follow a low-sodium, heart-healthy diet before the transplant greatly helped in my recovery from the surgery and will play a big part in my health going forward. I recovered from surgery very quickly and left the hospital on June 4, just nine days after the procedure was performed.

cont'd

With my new lease on life, I am looking forward to starting a family with my wife of two years, Mindy, and making the best of every moment. Also, I want to be able to help people struggling to change their eating habits realize that they, too, can be successful. This is the reason I have written this book filled with recipes and tips for heart-healthy living. Use it in good health!

# the
# introduction

In all likelihood, your doctor has told you to reduce the amount of sodium in your diet. Despite how difficult this may sound, it does not have to take the spice out of eating! With a positive outlook and some simple changes in your dietary habits, you can take charge of your health while continuing to enjoy tasty foods of all sorts – even snacks and desserts!

The first step is to realize you are not alone. Nearly everyone can benefit from reducing the amount of dietary salt. This may sound overwhelming, but it is really just a matter of educating yourself, making a plan, and slowly adjusting your habits to healthier ones. In this book, I will share tips I have learned and tried-and-true recipes I have created to help make this transition easier – and tastier – for you and your loved ones!

To start on the road to your healthier, low-sodium lifestyle, you first need to know exactly what is in the food you are eating. Begin by keeping a journal of the sodium content of the foods that you consume. After you are comfortable with tracking your sodium intake, you can add other nutritional facts that are important in your personal diet such as fat, cholesterol or fiber. It is much easier to hold yourself accountable when you can see this record on paper. To help you in this task, I have put together a simple explanation of how to read a food label and have included it in this book.

Armed with this new information, visit your grocery store to learn more about the foods you have been eating. I recommend doing this early on a Saturday or Sunday morning after breakfast when the store is typically less crowded. This "field trip" will make it easier to identify which products to buy and which products to avoid on future shopping excursions.

Back at home, go through your kitchen or pantry and get rid of everything that is high in sodium. This will mainly include processed foods, such as canned goods (unless they are "no salt added"), instant packaged dinners, most frozen meals, chips, and crackers. Discarding these high-sodium foods will help ease the temptation to go back to your old high-sodium habits.

Next, restock your kitchen or pantry with the products I have listed in this book as the "Top 20 Low-Sodium Staples to Keep on Hand." Make sure to keep your food selections heart-healthy all the way around. Not only should the foods be low in sodium, but they should also be low in fat, low in cholesterol, and high in fiber. Remember: Fresh is always the best way to go! Try to stay away from processed foods and canned vegetables. If canned vegetables are your only option, drain and rinse them well to help remove as much sodium as possible. You may be able to use salt substitutes, but check with your doctor before doing so because they may interfere with some medications.

If you are like me before I began my low-sodium lifestyle, I did not know where to begin in the kitchen, and that is how this book got started. To be successful, I knew I had to take charge of my eating habits, so I needed a plan that I could live with. Even though I have been blessed with outstanding doctors and a loving, supportive family, they can only do so much. After all, I alone am ultimately responsible for what goes into my mouth!

There are many low-sodium cookbooks available, but I sought out recipes that were easy to make and did not require expensive ingredients that could only be ordered online or purchased at specialty stores. I wanted the convenience of being to go to the local grocery store to buy ingredients for my dishes.

I began with some simple recipes that require only mixing a few ingredients and put them on the grill or in the oven. Next, I experimented with other foods I had always enjoyed and developed recipes that would make them as low in sodium as possible while still being tasty and fun to eat.

I started out with the "tools" most households have for food preparation: a stove, a microwave, and a gas grill. I realized that with a few additions, I would have more choices in cooking. I have since bought a charcoal grill because charcoal brings a different flavor in when you take out the salt. I have also purchased a slow cooker, which makes cooking easier and also brings out different flavors in the foods I prepare. Another great addition has been a bread maker. Some people joke about opening a beautifully wrapped gift only to find a bread maker, but I was truly excited when I got mine! My bread maker allows me to create delicious breads with no or very little sodium in them. Yet another great tool I enjoy using is a smoker, which brings out still different flavors in the foods I prepare.

As you grow comfortable in the kitchen and try your own creative approaches, turn on some of the cooking shows found on the various cable stations today. It is true that these shows can make you hungry, but I have picked up some valuable tips on food preparation and which ingredients go together by watching these experienced chefs.

Just like anything else, you have to make time for what is important, but I have learned ways to make low-sodium cooking easier and quicker. It just takes planning ahead. I have gotten into the habit of cooking at least once a day. I have found that it is often easier for me to cook in the evenings when I am not in as much of a hurry. I fix larger quantities so that I will have enough left over to eat the next day. On the weekends when I have more time, I often make salad dressings, sauces, and breads. I also cut up fruits and vegetables and use them in the week ahead so that I can prepare things more quickly when I am crunched for time.

Using steam bags is a very easy way to cook healthy foods quickly. Also, you may wish to buy a couple of empty squeeze bottles to use for salad dressings and sauces. Ketchup without salt added simply did not taste right to me at first, so I mixed it with regular ketchup in a squeeze bottle. This maintained the flavor I was used to while reducing the sodium.

Some low-sodium frozen dinners are fine to eat when you are in a hurry, but you have to be very selective. Look for dinners that have 600 mg of sodium or less. A low-sodium frozen entrée with a salad, piece of fruit, handful of low-sodium chips, or a slice of homemade bread can be a quick, healthy lunch or dinner.

I have found breakfast to be the hardest meal to eat when you are trying to limit your salt intake. Most traditional breakfast foods, such as bacon, sausage, milk, many dry cereals, breads, and pastries are laden with sodium. I always stick to oatmeal or dry cereal (there are a few varieties that have no sodium), yogurt, fruit, certain types of fiber bars, or a couple of egg whites.

If you like to eat out – and of course most of us do – only dine at places that provide nutritional information until you become more familiar with your low-sodium lifestyle. Some places have this information on display, while at other restaurants you will have to request it. In some cases, you can also find this information online. As you visit different restaurants, make it a new hobby to collect as much nutrition information as you can, and keep it in a folder in your car for quick access when you are dining on the go. Try to know what you can eat at certain restaurants ahead of time so that when you get there you will not be tempted to order some-thing you should not. When you arrive at the restaurant and the aroma is in the air, it is much tougher to do the right thing if you haven't planned in advance!

After looking at nutrition guides from various restaurants, you will learn there can be quite a difference in nutrition facts in something as simple as a hamburger. You will notice that restau-rants season the meat differently, and you will also find differences in the sodium content of their buns and toppings.

Without a doubt, it is challenging to watch your sodium when dining out, but it can be done! Here are a few suggestions I can offer to help you out:

- Try to stay away from things that are covered in sauces.
- If you order a steak, ask for no seasoning.
- When ordering a salad, see if they can leave off the high-sodium ingredients, such as olives, cheese, and bacon. Ask for salad dressing on the side, and dip your fork in the dressing before taking a bite.
- Ask for steamed vegetables with no butter or seasonings.
- Try to skip or limit the breads, as these are usually high in sodium.
- If you go to a place with a salad bar, try to eat more vegetables, fruits, and low-sodium options from the bar, and balance it out with a smaller meal. I love pizza, but I have not found a low-sodium pizza place. Therefore, I choose a pizza restaurant with a salad bar and eat a couple platefuls of salad with just two or three slices of pizza.

Again, it's all about planning! Try to decide what you are going to eat before you get to the restaurant, and try to eat your other meals that day with the least amount of sodium possible. If your doctor says, for example, that your daily sodium level should not exceed 2000 mg, this does not mean you can not enjoy an occasional treat. **Remember:** Moderation is key! Just try to balance out any "splurges" at some other point in the day!

It will probably take a couple of weeks before you really begin to "taste" food. Most people eat so much sodium that their taste buds are altered to distinguish only salt. Once you give your low-sodium diet a chance and track your salt intake for a few days, you will be amazed at the progress you are making and how much better you feel. I firmly believe that learning how to eat this way – and help from up above – saved my life and allowed me to be fortunate enough to have a heart transplant.

I had to begin my low-sodium lifestyle nearly four years ago, and learned the hard way as far as what worked, what didn't, and the best ways to make necessary adjustments. Today, when I put salty food up to my mouth, I can actually feel how my chest felt when I ate too much sodium in the past. It was like to breathing with concrete blocks on my chest.

Keeping my salt intake down while awaiting my transplant allowed me to be more physically active, and when I found that out, it became my motivation to continue my regimen. Eating the salty foods just was not worth it. Eliminating them helped me to be able to keep doing things most people take for granted, like simply walking around. In fact, I was even able to continue other physical activities I enjoyed, such as playing volleyball and cutting the grass.

During the months before my transplant, I had reduced my sodium intake to 1000 mg or less per day. I believe this drastic reduction allowed me to do things physically that doctors told me I should not be able to do based on my cardiac catheterization results. Other heart patients with the same results could not do the things I could do physically. I had some doctors scratching their heads, wondering how I could still maintain the intensity of my activity level, so I had to prove what I could do on a treadmill to the doctor.

Your reason for following a low-sodium diet will probably be different than mine. But regardless of your specific circumstances, I believe you can benefit from the tips I have learned and the low-sodium recipes I have developed. Take the recipes in this book, and tweak them to your liking. If you like garlic, add more. If you don't like red pepper flakes, leave them out. You will find the combination that works for you – and feel better for it in the long run.

It all comes down to this: You must break old, unhealthy habits and exchange them for new, healthier ones. Take the information in this book, and be empowered. You'll be amazed at how better you will feel. I firmly believe that if I can do it, you can do it too!

# Equipping
## your kitchen

## Gadgets

Scale *(controlling portion size is important)*
2 Sets of measuring cups and measuring spoons *(one set is always dirty)*
Meat thermometer *(makes it easier to tell when meat is done)*
Mandolin slicer *(makes cutting easier and cuts food equal size for even cooking)*
Hand held mixer *(takes up less room)*
Small food processor *(or a larger one if you have the room)*
Hand Blender

Bread Machine
Toaster Oven
Slow cooker
Smoker
Grill
Blender

## Cooking Vessels

Baking sheets
12 cup muffin tin
Small and large non-stick skillet
Small, medium, large pots with lids
Casserole dishes
   *(various sizes  9" X 13", 8" x 8")*
6 quart pot
9" x 13" baking pan

9" x 5" loaf pan
Glass measuring cups
2 cutting boards
   *(one for raw meat, one for everything else)*
Colander
2-3 different size mixing bowls

## Utensils

Several good basic sharp knives
   *(chefs knife, bread knife, paring knife,
   slicing knife and filet knife)*
2-3 Spatulas
   *(once again, one is always dirty)*
Whisks
Vegetable peeler
Box grater with different size holes
Can Opener

Meat tenderizer
Tongs
Cork screw
Pizza cutter
Ladle
Different size spoons
Basting brush
Metal skewers

# Top 20
## Low Sodium
### Cooking Staples
### to have on hand

1. NSA* Ketchup
2. NSA* Tomato Paste
3. NSA* Tomato Sauce
4. Plain Panko Bread Crumbs
5. Potatoes and Sweet Potatoes
6. Onions
7. Garlic
8. Olive and Canola Oil
9. Chicken Breast
10. Ground Beef or Turkey
11. White And Red Wine Vinegar
12. Light Sour Cream
13. Light Mayonnaise

14. Horseradish
15. Lemon Juice
16. White and Brown Sugar
17. Unsalted Butter
18. Whole Grain Brown Rice
19. Flour
20. Some basic spices:
    - ☑ Garlic Powder
    - ☑ Onion Powder
    - ☑ Basil
    - ☑ Parsley
    - ☑ Oregano
    - ☑ Thyme
    - ☑ Paprika
    - ☑ Chili Powder
    - ☑ Cumin

*NSA - No Sodium Added

# Reading a
# food label

## Nutrition Facts
Serving Size 2 crackers (14 g)
Serving Per Container About 21

Amount Per Serving

**Calories** 60   Calories from Fat 15

| | % Daily Value* |
|---|---|
| **Total Fat** 1.5 g | 2% |
| Saturated Fat 0g | 0% |
| Trans Fat 0g | |
| **Cholesterol** 0 mg | 0% |
| **Sodium** 70mg | 3% |
| **Total Carbohydrate** 10g | 3% |
| Dietary Fiber Less than 1g | 3% |
| Sugars 0g | |
| **Protein** 2g | |

Vitamin A 0%  •  Vitamin C 0%

Calcium 0%  •  Iron 2%

\* Percent Daily Values are based on a 2,000 calorie diet. Your daily values may be higher or lower depending on your calorie needs:

| | Calories | 2,000 | 2,500 |
|---|---|---|---|
| Total Fat | Less than | 66g | 80g |
| Sat Fat | Less than | 20g | 25g |
| Cholesterol | Less than | 300mg | 300mg |
| Sodium | Less than | 2400mg | 2400mg |
| Total Carbohydrate | | 300mg | 375mg |
| Dietary Fiber | | 25g | 30g |

**1.**

**2.**

**3.**

**4.**

**5.**

**6.**

**7.**

**8.**

**9.**

**1. Serving Size** – Look at this first, as it can be deceiving. The serving size is usually based on the amount of food people typically eat. Therefore, you need to compare the label serving size with the amount you actually eat. For example, if the label says 70 mg of sodium per serving, you may think it is not much. But when you multiply that number by the amount of the food you actually eat or need for a recipe, it soon turns into a lot. Always multiply or divide this amount if you eat more or less than what the label states as a serving.

**2. Calories and Calories from Fat** – This is what counts if you are trying to lose or maintain your weight. Food labels are based on a 2,000 or 2,500 - calorie diet. Dietitians recommend looking for foods with less than 30 percent of calories coming from fat.

**3. Total Fat** – This is the number of fat grams contained in one serving of the food. The different kinds of fat, such as saturated, unsaturated, and trans fat, will be listed separately. Everybody needs fat in their diet. You just want to eat less of the saturated and trans fat.

**4. Cholesterol** – Try to limit this amount to 200 mg or less per day.

**5. Sodium** – This is the amount of salt in the food. (My doctor restricted my sodium to 2000 mg per day.)

**6. Total Carbohydrates** – Carbohydrates are in the breads, pastas, rice, starchy vegetables, fruits, and sweets you eat. If you have issues with diabetes, pay special attention to carbohydrate grams, not just sugars.

**7. Dietary Fiber** – Try to get 25 to 30 mg per day of dietary fiber. This may help you lower your cholesterol while improving or preventing constipation, slowing digestion, and making you feel full longer.

**8. Sugar** – Sugar adds calories and carbohydrates. It is often labeled under "alias" names ending in "ose" or "trin"

**9. Protein** – This number tells you how much protein you get from a single serving of the food. Most Americans get more protein than they need, so a % Daily Value is not required on product labels.

# More
# about this book:

 **Shop Around:** This grocery store symbol may be next to various ingredients through out the book. You will find that all brands of a particular ingredient contain a wide range of sodium. I recommend shopping around at your local store to find the brand that is lowest in sodium. Often the store's own brand may have the lowest sodium content.

 **f.y.i. tips:** These tips are included on some recipes to give further ideas on lowering sodium, making a recipe faster, or to give general food preparation knowledge.

 **Carbohydrate X-change:** These Exchange numbers are listed in the bottom corner of every recipe page for those who are controlling their blood sugar. Each Carb X-change = 15 carbohydrates.

 **Total Sodium:** The total sodium amounts per serving are listed in the bottom corner of every recipe page for a quick reference. Also, you will find total sodium content per serving across from each ingredient.

 **NSA:** No Sodium Added. There are many NSA products available in your local supermarket. You will often see this acronym beside ingredients in my recipes.

 **Food Scale:** I recommend buying a small kitchen scale for weighing food. This will help you better manage sodium content.

# season
# it

# Jerk Seasoning (Rub)

**Mix & Store:**

## Ingredients:

| | Sodium per serving |
|---|---|
| 2 Tbsp. Dried Minced Onion | <1mg |
| 1 Tbsp. Sugar | 0mg |
| 2½ tsp. Thyme | 0mg |
| 2 tsp. Garlic Powder | <1mg |
| 1½ tsp. Black Pepper | 0mg |
| 1½ tsp. All Spice | 0mg |
| 1 tsp. Red Pepper Flakes | 0mg |
| 1 tsp. Cayenne Pepper | 0mg |
| ½ tsp. Dried Chives | <1mg |
| ¼ tsp. Cinnamon | 0mg |
| ¼ tsp. Nutmeg | 0mg |
| ¼ tsp. Ground Cloves | 0mg |
| ⅛ tsp. Tumeric | 0mg |

## How to:

Combine all ingredients in a small container.

**Suggestion:** Could be used to season chicken or pork chops.

Yields:  20 servings  (1 serving = 1 tsp.)

## fyi:

**Sugar:** For a healthier recipe, an equivalent sugar substitute may be substituted for sugar.

| Cal | Tot Fat | Sat Fat | Chol. | Potass | Carbs | Prot. | Fiber | Sugar |
|---|---|---|---|---|---|---|---|---|
| 6 | <1g | 0g | 0mg | 14mg | 2g | <1g | <1g | <1g |

CARB X-change 0

Total Sodium per serving <1mg

# Italian Seasoning

## Ingredients:

| | Sodium per serving |
|---|---|
| 2 Tbsp. Dried Basil | 0mg |
| 2 Tbsp. Dried Oregano | 0mg |
| 2 Tbsp. Dried Thyme | 0mg |
| 2 Tbsp. Marjoram | 0mg |
| 1 Tbsp. Dried Rosemary | 0mg |
| 1 Tbsp. Dried Sage | 0mg |
| 2 tsp. Garlic Powder | <1mg |
| 1 tsp. Onion Powder | <1mg |

## How to:

Combine all ingredients in a small container.

**Suggestion:** Could be used to season chicken or pork chops.

Yields: 12 servings (1 serving = 1 tsp.)

| Cal | Tot Fat | Sat Fat | Chol. | Potass | Carbs | Prot. | Fiber | Sugar |
|---|---|---|---|---|---|---|---|---|
| 3 | <1g | 0g | 0mg | 13mg | <1g | <1g | <1g | <1g |

CARB X-change
0

Total Sodium per serving
<1mg

# Taco Seasoning Mix

**Mix & Store:**

### Ingredients:

| | Sodium per serving |
|---|---|
| 1½ Tbsp. Flour | <1mg |
| 1 Tbsp. Chili Powder | 76mg |
| ½ tsp. Paprika | <1mg |
| 1 tsp. Dried Minced Onion | <1mg |
| ½ tsp. Cumin | 2mg |
| 1 tsp. Garlic Powder | <1mg |
| ¼ tsp. Sugar | 0mg |
| ¼ tsp. Oregano | <1mg |
| ¼ tsp. Cayenne Pepper | 0mg |
| ¼ tsp. Black Pepper | 0mg |

### How to:

Combine all ingredients in a small container.

When ready to use, add ⅔ cup water to mix. Seasons 1 lb. of meat.

Yields: 7 servings (1 serving = 1 tsp.)

**fyi:**

**Chili Powder:** A no sodium chili powder is available in specialty stores or see recipe on page 5.

**Sugar:** For a healthier recipe, an equivalent sugar substitute may be substituted for sugar.

| Cal | Tot Fat | Sat Fat | Chol. | Potass | Carbs | Prot. | Fiber | Sugar |
|---|---|---|---|---|---|---|---|---|
| 102 | 2g | <1g | 0mg | 253mg | 23g | 3g | 4g | 6g |

CARB X-change 1½

Total Sodium per serving <1mg

# Classic Chili Powder

## Ingredients:

| | Sodium per serving |
|---|---|
| 3 Tbsp. Paprika | <1mg |
| 2 tsp. Oregano | <1mg |
| 1½ tsp. Cumin | <1mg |
| 1 tsp. Tumeric | 0mg |
| 1½ tsp. Garlic Powder | 0mg |
| ½ tsp. Cayenne Pepper | 0mg |

## How to:

Combine all ingredients in a small container.

Yields: 15 servings (1 serving = 1 tsp.)

### fyi:
Use in place of store bought chili powder.

| Cal | Tot Fat | Sat Fat | Chol. | Potass | Carbs | Prot. | Fiber | Sugar |
|---|---|---|---|---|---|---|---|---|
| 7 | <1g | 0g | 0mg | 44mg | 1g | <1g | <1g | <1g |

CARB X-change 0

Total Sodium per serving <1mg

# Italian Dressing Mix

## Ingredients:

| | Sodium per serving |
|---|---|
| 2 Tbsp. Oregano | <1mg |
| 1 Tbsp. Onion Powder | <1mg |
| 1 Tbsp. Garlic Powder | <1mg |
| 1 Tbsp. Sugar | 0mg |
| 1 Tbsp. Dried Parsley | <1mg |
| 1 tsp. Black Pepper | 0mg |
| 1 tsp. Basil | 0mg |
| ½ tsp. Red Pepper Flakes | 0mg |
| ¼ tsp. Marjoram | 0mg |
| ¼ tsp. Celery Seed | 0mg |

## How to:

Combine all ingredients in a small container.

Yields:  20 servings  (1 serving = 1 tsp.)

## fyi:

**Sugar:** For a healthier recipe, an equivalent sugar substitute may be substituted for sugar.

| Cal | Tot Fat | Sat Fat | Chol. | Potass | Carbs | Prot. | Fiber | Sugar |
|---|---|---|---|---|---|---|---|---|
| 7 | <1g | 0g | 0mg | 34mg | 2g | <1g | <1g | 1g |

CARB X-change
0

Total Sodium per serving
<1mg

# BBQ Rub

## Ingredients:

| | Sodium per serving |
|---|---|
| ¼ cup Brown Sugar | 0mg |
| ¼ cup Sugar | 0mg |
| 2 Tbsp. Paprika | 0mg |
| 1½ Tbsp. Garlic Powder | <1mg |
| 1 Tbsp. Mustard Powder | <1mg |
| ½ Tbsp. Onion Powder | <1mg |
| ½ Tbsp. Rosemary | 0mg |
| ½ Tbsp. Black Pepper | 0mg |
| ½ Tbsp. Cayenne Pepper (optional) | 0mg |

## How to:

Combine all ingredients in a small container.

**Suggestion:** Can be used to season chicken or pork chops. Also, wonderful on a pork butt in a smoker.

Yields:  30 servings  (1 serving = 1 tsp.)

---

**fyi:**

**Sugar and Brown Sugar:** For a healthier recipe, an equivalent sugar substitute or brown sugar substitute may be substituted for sugar.

---

| Cal | Tot Fat | Sat Fat | Chol. | Potass | Carbs | Prot. | Fiber | Sugar |
|---|---|---|---|---|---|---|---|---|
| 17 | 0g | 0g | 0mg | 26mg | 5g | <1g | <1g | 4g |

CARB X-change: 0

Total Sodium per serving: 1mg

# dressings

# Catalina Dressing

## Ingredients:

| | Sodium per serving |
|---|---|
| ½ cup Sugar | 0mg |
| ¼ tsp. Paprika | 0mg |
| ¼ tsp. Black Pepper | 0mg |
| ¼ tsp. Ground Mustard | 0mg |
| ¼ tsp. Celery Seed | 0mg |
| 1 Tbsp. Onion, grated | 0mg |
| ¼ cup White Wine Vinegar | 0mg |
| ⅓ cup NSA Ketchup | 1mg |
| ½ cup Canola Oil | 0mg |

## How to:

Place all ingredients in a jar or blender and mix well.

Refrigerate to store.

Yields: Approx. 24 servings (1 serving = 1 Tbsp.)

## fyi:

**Sugar:** For a healthier recipe, an equivalent sugar substitute may be substituted for sugar.

| Cal | Tot Fat | Sat Fat | Chol. | Potass | Carbs | Prot. | Fiber | Sugar |
|---|---|---|---|---|---|---|---|---|
| 6 | 5g | <1g | 0mg | 39mg | 6g | 0g | 0g | 5g |

CARB X-change ½

Total Sodium per serving
1mg

# Ranch Dressing

## Ingredients:

| | Sodium per serving |
|---|---|
| ½ cup Skim Milk | 5mg |
| ½ Tbsp. Lemon Juice | 0mg |
| ½ cup Light Mayonnaise 🛒 | 40mg |
| ⅓ cup Light Sour Cream 🛒 | 6mg |
| ½ tsp. Vegetable Oil | 0mg |
| ½ tsp. Garlic Powder | 0mg |
| 1 tsp. Dried Chives | 0mg |
| ½ tsp. Dried Parsley | 0mg |
| ½ tsp. Dill Weed | 0mg |
| ½ tsp. Onion Powder | 0mg |
| A pinch of Black Pepper | 0mg |

## How to:

Combine milk and lemon juice in a small bowl and let stand for 10 minutes.

In another bowl, whisk together remaining ingredients and add milk/lemon juice to mixture.

Refrigerate to store.

Yields: 12 servings (1 serving = 1 Tbsp.)

## fyi:

**Mayonnaise:** I have found the store brand is generally lower in sodium.

| Cal | Tot Fat | Sat Fat | Chol. | Potass | Carbs | Prot. | Fiber | Sugar |
|---|---|---|---|---|---|---|---|---|
| 43 | 4g | 1g | 2mg | 22mg | 2g | <1g | 0g | <1g |

CARB X-change 0

Total Sodium per serving 51mg

# Thousand Island

## Ingredients:

|  | Sodium per serving |
|---|---|
| ¼ cup Light Mayonnaise 🛒 | 24mg |
| 2 Tbsp. NSA Ketchup | 0mg |
| 1 Tbsp. White Vinegar | 0mg |
| 1½ tsp. Sugar | 0mg |
| 1 Tbsp. Sweet Relish 🛒 | 12mg |
| 1 Tbsp. Onion, finely minced | 0mg |

## How to:

Mix all ingredients in a small bowl.

Refrigerate to store.

Yields:  10 servings  (1 serving = 1 Tbsp.)

## fyi:

**Sugar:**  For a healthier recipe, an equivalent sugar substitute may be substituted for sugar.

**Mayonnaise:**  I have found the store brand is generally lower in sodium.

| Cal | Tot Fat | Sat Fat | Chol. | Potass | Carbs | Prot. | Fiber | Sugar |
|---|---|---|---|---|---|---|---|---|
| 23 | 1g | <1g | 0mg | 2mg | 3g | 0g | 0g | 2g |

CARB X-change 0

Total Sodium per serving 36mg

# Poppy Seed Dressing

## Ingredients:

| | Sodium per serving |
|---|---|
| ⅓ cup Sugar | 0mg |
| 2½ tsp. Cider Vinegar | 0mg |
| 2 tsp. Onion, finely chopped | <1mg |
| 1½ tsp. Mustard Powder | 0mg |
| 1 tsp. Poppy Seeds | 0mg |
| ½ cup Canola Oil | 0mg |

## How to:

Combine all ingredients except oil in a small bowl or jar.

Slowly whisk in oil or add to jar and shake well.

Yields: 16 servings  (1 serving = 1 Tbsp.)

**fyi:**

**Sugar:**  For a healthier recipe, an equivalent sugar substitute may be substituted for sugar.

| Cal | Tot Fat | Sat Fat | Chol. | Potass | Carbs | Prot. | Fiber | Sugar |
|---|---|---|---|---|---|---|---|---|
| 78 | 7g | <1g | 0mg | 3mg | 4g | 0g | 0g | 4g |

CARB X-change 0

Total Sodium per serving <1mg

# Honey Mustard Dressing

## Ingredients:

| | Sodium per serving |
|---|---|
| ¼ cup Light Mayonnaise  | 24mg |
| 1 Tbsp. Mustard | 21mg |
| 1½ Tbsp. Honey | <1mg |
| 1 tsp. Lemon Juice | 0mg |

## How to:

Mix all ingredients in a small bowl.

Refrigerate to store.

Yields: 8 servings (1 serving = 1 Tbsp.)

---

**fyi:**

**Mayonnaise:** I have found the store brand is generally lower in sodium.

---

| Cal | Tot Fat | Sat Fat | Chol. | Potass | Carbs | Prot. | Fiber | Sugar |
|---|---|---|---|---|---|---|---|---|
| 27 | 2g | <1g | 0mg | 6mg | 4g | <1g | <1g | 3g |

CARB X-change **0**

Total Sodium per serving 45mg

# Red Wine Vinaigrette

**Just Mix:**

## Ingredients:

| Ingredient | Sodium per serving |
|---|---|
| 3½ Tbsp. Red Wine Vinegar | 0mg |
| 1 tsp. Honey Dijon Mustard  | 3mg |
| 1 tsp. Sugar | 0mg |
| ½ tsp. Dried Basil | 0mg |
| ½ tsp. Garlic, minced | 0mg |
| ¼ tsp. Poppy Seeds | 0mg |
| ½ cup Extra Virgin Olive Oil | 0mg |

## How to:

Combine all ingredients except oil in a small bowl or jar.

Slowly whisk in oil or add to jar and shake well.

Yields: 12 servings (1 serving = 1 Tbsp.)

---

**fyi:**

**Sugar:** For a healthier recipe, an equivalent sugar substitute may be substituted for sugar.

---

| Cal | Tot Fat | Sat Fat | Chol. | Potass | Carbs | Prot. | Fiber | Sugar |
|---|---|---|---|---|---|---|---|---|
| 92 | 9g | 1g | 0mg | 5mg | 7g | 0g | 0g | 1g |

CARB X-change 0

Total Sodium per serving 3mg

# Balsamic Vinaigrette

## Ingredients:

|  | Sodium per serving |
|---|---|
| 2½ Tbsp. Balsamic Vinegar | 1mg |
| 1 tsp. Honey Dijon Mustard | 5mg |
| 1 tsp. Brown Sugar | <1mg |
| ½ tsp. Black Pepper | <1mg |
| ½ tsp. Garlic, minced | <1mg |
| ⅓ cup Extra Virgin Olive Oil | 0mg |

## How to:

Combine all ingredients except oil in a small bowl or jar.

Slowly whisk in oil or add to jar and shake well.

Yields: 10 servings (1 serving = 1 Tbsp.)

## fyi:

**Brown Sugar:** For a healthier recipe, an equivalent brown sugar substitute may be substituted for brown sugar.

| Cal | Tot Fat | Sat Fat | Chol. | Potass | Carbs | Prot. | Fiber | Sugar |
|---|---|---|---|---|---|---|---|---|
| 69 | 7g | 1g | 0mg | 4mg | 1g | <1g | 0g | 2g |

CARB X-change ½

Total Sodium per serving
6mg

# French Dressing

## Ingredients:

| | Sodium per serving |
|---|---|
| ½ cup Vegetable Oil | 5mg |
| 3 Tbsp. White Wine Vinegar | 0mg |
| ¼ cup Sugar | 0mg |
| 2 Tbsp. NSA Ketchup | 40mg |
| ½ tsp. Worcestershire Sauce  | 6mg |
| ¼ cup Onion, finely minced | 0mg |

## How to:

Combine all ingredients except oil in a small bowl or jar.

Slowly whisk in oil or add to jar and shake well.

Yields: 12 servings (1 serving = 1 Tbsp.)

## fyi:

**Sugar:** For a healthier recipe, an equivalent sugar substitute may be substituted for sugar.

| Cal | Tot Fat | Sat Fat | Chol. | Potass | Carbs | Prot. | Fiber | Sugar |
|---|---|---|---|---|---|---|---|---|
| 43 | 4g | 1g | 2mg | 22mg | 2g | <1g | 0g | <1g |

CARB X-change 0

Total Sodium per serving 51mg

# Italian Dressing

Just Mix:

## Ingredients:

| | Sodium per serving |
|---|---|
| ⅓ cup White Wine Vinegar | 0mg |
| ⅔ cup Canola Oil | 0mg |
| 1 Tbsp. Water | 0mg |
| 2 Tbsp. Italian Dressing Mix, (See recipe on page 6.) | <1mg |
| 1 Tbsp. Grated Parmesan Cheese | 0mg |
| 1 Tbsp. Red Pepper Flakes | 0mg |

## How to:

Add all ingredients in a small bowl or container and whisk or shake container very well to combine.

Yields: 10 servings  (1 serving = 1 Tbsp.)

| Cal | Tot Fat | Sat Fat | Chol. | Potass | Carbs | Prot. | Fiber | Sugar |
|---|---|---|---|---|---|---|---|---|
| 134 | 15g | 1g | <1mg | 11mg | <1g | <1g | <1g | <1g |

CARB X-change
0

Total Sodium
10mg per serving

# it's in the
# **sauce**

# Cocktail Sauce

## Ingredients:

| | Sodium per serving |
|---|---|
| ¾ cup NSA Ketchup | 5mg |
| 2 Tbsp. Prepared Horseradish, Or to taste | 6mg |
| 2 tsp. Brown Sugar, packed | 0mg |
| 1 Tbsp. Lemon Juice | 0mg |
| 1 tsp. Garlic Powder | 0mg |

## How to:

Combine all ingredients in a small bowl. Taste and adjust horseradish to your liking.

Refrigerate to store.

Yields: 16  (1 serving = 1 Tbsp.)

## fyi:

A low Sodium **Horseradish** can be found in the dairy section of your store.

**Note:** Sodium content will change with amount of Horseradish.

**Brown Sugar:** For a healthier recipe, an equivalent brown sugar substitute may be substituted for brown sugar.

| Cal | Tot Fat | Sat Fat | Chol. | Potass | Carbs | Prot. | Fiber | Sugar |
|---|---|---|---|---|---|---|---|---|
| 23 | 0g | 0g | 0mg | 137mg | 6g | <1g | <1g | 3g |

CARB X-change ½

Total Sodium per serving 10mg

# Horseradish Sauce

## Ingredients:

| | Sodium per serving |
|---|---|
| ½ Tbsp. White Vinegar | 0mg |
| 2 tsp. Sugar | 0mg |
| ⅓ cup Light Mayonnaise  | 32mg |
| 2 Tbsp. Light Sour Cream | 3mg |
| 1 Tbsp + 1 tsp. Prepared Horseradish Or to taste | 6mg |

## How to:

Combine all ingredients in a small bowl.

Taste and adjust horseradish to your liking.

Yields: Approx. 10 (1 serving = 1 Tbsp.)

## fyi:

A low Sodium **Horseradish** can be found in the dairy section of your store.

**Note:** Sodium content will change with amount of Horseradish.

**Mayonnaise:** I have found the store brand is generally lower in sodium.

**Sugar:** For a healthier recipe, an equivalent sugar substitute may be substituted for sugar.

| Cal | Tot Fat | Sat Fat | Chol. | Potass | Carbs | Prot. | Fiber | Sugar |
|---|---|---|---|---|---|---|---|---|
| 27 | 2g | <1g | 1mg | 5mg | 2g | <1g | 0g | 1g |

Total Sodium per serving 41mg

# Chicken Gravy

## Ingredients:

| | Sodium per serving |
|---|---|
| 2 Tbsp. Unsalted Butter | <1mg |
| 2 Tbsp. All-Purpose Flour | 0mg |
| ¼ tsp. Pepper | 0mg |
| 1 cup of Chicken Drippings or  Low-Sodium Chicken Broth | 23mg |

**fyi:**

**Chicken Broth:** For an even lower sodium gravy use the recipe on page 27.

## How to:

Melt unsalted butter.

Add flour and pepper, and mix well.

Slowly add broth.

Heat on low, stirring until gravy thickens.

Yields:  Approx. 20 servings
(1 serving = 1 Tbsp.)

| Cal | Tot Fat | Sat Fat | Chol. | Potass | Carbs | Prot. | Fiber | Sugar |
|---|---|---|---|---|---|---|---|---|
| 33 | 1g | <1g | 3mg | 7mg | 5g | 1g | <1g | 0g |

Total Sodium
23mg per serving

# Chipotle Mayo

## Ingredients:

|  | Sodium per serving |
|---|---|
| ½ cup Mayonnaise | 60mg |
| 2 Chipotle Peppers in Adobo Sauce | 31mg |
| 2 tsp. Lime Juice | <1mg |
| 1 tsp. Garlic Powder | <1mg |

## How to:

Combine all ingredients in a small bowl.

Refrigerate.

Yields: 8 servings (1 serving = 1 Tbsp.)

---

**fyi:**

**Mayonnaise:** I have found the store brand is generally lower in sodium.

---

| Cal | Tot Fat | Sat Fat | Chol. | Potass | Carbs | Prot. | Fiber | Sugar |
|---|---|---|---|---|---|---|---|---|
| 37 | 4g | <1g | 0mg | 3mg | 2g | 0g | <1g | 0g |

CARB X-change 0

Total Sodium per serving 91mg

# HOT Taco Sauce

## Ingredients:

| | Sodium per serving |
|---|---|
| 8 oz. NSA Tomato Sauce | 3mg |
| ⅓ cup Water | 0mg |
| ¼ tsp. Chili Powder  | <1mg |
| ½ Tbsp. Cumin | <1mg |
| ½ Tbsp. Dried Minced Onion | <1mg |
| 1 Tbsp. White Vinegar | 0mg |
| ½ tsp Garlic Powder | <1mg |
| ¼ tsp. Paprika | 0mg |
| ¼ tsp. Sugar | 0mg |
| ¼ tsp. Cayenne Pepper, (or to taste) | 0mg |

## How to:

Mix all ingredients in a small saucepan.

Simmer 20-25 minutes.

Will keep in refrigerator for about a week.

Yields:  20  (1 serving = 1 Tbsp.)

## fyi:

**Chili Powder:** A no sodium chili powder is available in specialty stores or see recipe on page 5.

**Sugar:** For a healthier recipe, an equivalent sugar substitute may be substituted for sugar.

| Cal | Tot Fat | Sat Fat | Chol. | Potass | Carbs | Prot. | Fiber | Sugar |
|---|---|---|---|---|---|---|---|---|
| 6 | 0g | 0g | 0mg | 15mg | 1g | <1g | <1g | <1g |

CARB X-change 0

Total Sodium per serving 4mg

# Memphis Style BBQ Sauce

## Ingredients:

| | Sodium per serving |
|---|---|
| 1 Tbsp. Olive Oil | 0mg |
| ½ cup Onion, chopped | 0mg |
| 5 Garlic Cloves, chopped | 3mg |
| 2 cups NSA Ketchup | 0mg |
| ½ cup Cider Vinegar | 0mg |
| ½ cup Dark Brown Sugar, packed | 5mg |
| 2 Tbsp. Worcestershire Sauce 🛒 | 20mg |
| 2 Tbsp. Lemon Juice | 0mg |
| 2 Tbsp. Honey | 0mg |
| 2 Tbsp. Dry Mustard | 0mg |
| ½ tsp. Black Pepper | 0mg |
| ¼ tsp. Cayenne Pepper | 0mg |

## How to:

In a medium sauce pan, combine oil, garlic, and onion and cook about 5 minutes until garlic and onion soften.

Add remaining ingredients, and simmer for 15-20 minutes.

Strain out onion and garlic before eating, if desired.

Yields: 2½ cups. (30 Tbsp.)
(1 serving = 1 Tbsp.)

## fyi:

**Dark Brown Sugar:** For a healthier recipe, a light brown sugar or a brown sugar substitute equivalent may be substituted for the dark brown sugar.

| Cal | Tot Fat | Sat Fat | Chol. | Potass | Carbs | Prot. | Fiber | Sugar |
|---|---|---|---|---|---|---|---|---|
| 73 | <1g | 0g | 0mg | 289mg | 17g | 0g | 0g | 5g |

CARB X-change 1

Total Sodium per serving 28mg

# Tartar Sauce

## Ingredients:

| | Sodium per serving |
|---|---|
| ½ cup Light Mayonnaise | 48mg |
| 1 Tbsp. Onion, minced | 0mg |
| 1 Tbsp. Low Sodium Sweet Relish | 10mg |
| ½ tsp. Lemon Juice | 0mg |
| 1½ tsp. Sugar | 0mg |

## How to:

Mix all ingredients in a small bowl.

Refrigerate to store.

Yields: Approx. 10 servings
(1 serving = 1 Tbsp.)

### fyi:

**Mayonnaise:** I have found the store brand is generally lower in sodium.

**Sugar:** For a healthier recipe, an equivalent sugar substitute may be substituted for sugar.

☑ SUPER EASY

| Cal | Tot Fat | Sat Fat | Chol. | Potass | Carbs | Prot. | Fiber | Sugar |
|---|---|---|---|---|---|---|---|---|
| 33 | 3g | <1g | 0mg | 4mg | 2g | 0g | 0g | <1g |

CARB X-change 0

Total Sodium 58mg per serving

# Chicken Broth

## Ingredients:

**2 Gallons + 1½ cups Water,** divided

**4 Carrots,** peeled and roughly chopped

**4 Celery Stalks,** including leaves, roughly chopped

**3 Garlic Cloves,** peeled and crushed

**1 Large Onion,** roughly chopped

**2 Bay Leaves**

**8-10 Whole Peppercorns**

**5-6 Fresh Thyme Sprigs**

**10 Sprigs Fresh Parsley,** with stems

**1 Whole Chicken,** cut into 9 pieces

## How to:

In a large stock pot, pour in 2 gallons of water and combine remaining ingredients and bring to a boil.

Simmer for 2 hours then pour remaining 1½ cups of water in pot. Skim off any fat from top and continue to simmer for another 1 to 1½ hours.

Remove chicken and let cool.

Strain broth into clean storage container.

Let cool overnight in refrigerator and skim fat off before use.

Remove meat from bones and reserve for later use.

**Suggestion:** Freeze broth in ½ - 1 cup containers for easy use.

Yields: 14 servings  (1 serving = 1 cup)

| Cal | Tot Fat | Sat Fat | Chol. | Potass | Carbs | Prot. | Fiber | Sugar |
|-----|---------|---------|-------|--------|-------|-------|-------|-------|
| 20 | 5g | 5g | 6mg | 0mg | 1g | 0g | 0g | 1g |

CARB X-change 0

Total Sodium 60mg per serving

# Classic Tomato Sauce

On The Stove:

## Ingredients:

| | Sodium per serving |
|---|---|
| 2 Tbsp. Extra Virgin Olive Oil | 0mg |
| 1 cup Onion, minced | 0mg |
| 4 Garlic Cloves, minced | <1mg |
| 2 - 14.5 oz. cans NSA Diced Tomatoes | 70mg |
| 1 - 6 oz. can of NSA Tomato Paste | 25mg |
| 1 Tbsp. Sugar | 0mg |
| 1 tsp. Dried Basil or 1 Tbsp. Fresh Basil | 0mg |
| ½ tsp. Dried Oregano or ½ Tbsp. Fresh Oregano | 0mg |
| ½ tsp. Black Pepper | 0mg |
| Parsley | 0mg |
| 1 Bay Leaf | 0mg |

## How to:

In a medium sauce pan, add olive oil, onion, and garlic, and cook until soft.

Add tomatoes and remaining ingredients to pan, and simmer on low for about an hour, stirring occasionally.

**Suggestion:** For a thinner sauce, chop or pulse tomatoes in food processor.

Yields: 8 servings (1 serving = ½ cup)

## fyi:

**Sugar:** For a healthier recipe, an equivalent sugar substitute may be substituted for sugar.

☑ FAMILY FAVORITE

| Cal | Tot Fat | Sat Fat | Chol. | Potass | Carbs | Prot. | Fiber | Sugar |
|---|---|---|---|---|---|---|---|---|
| 85 | 4g | <1g | 0mg | 249mg | 12g | 8g | 3g | 7g |

CARB X-change 1

Total Sodium per serving
95mg

# Jamaican Jerk Sauce

## Ingredients:

| Ingredient | Sodium per serving |
|---|---|
| 3 Tbsp. Unsalted Butter | <1mg |
| 2 Tbsp. Green Onion, finely chopped | <1mg |
| ¾ cup Water | <1mg |
| ¾ cup NSA Ketchup | 0mg |
| ½ cup Light Brown Sugar, packed | 0mg |
| ¼ cup Vinegar | 0mg |
| 2 Tbsp. Hot Sauce | 6mg |
| 2 Tbsp. Molasses | <1mg |
| 1 Tbsp. Cornstarch | 0mg |
| 2 tsp. Worcestershire Sauce | 3mg |
| 2 tsp. Lemon Juice | 0mg |
| 1 tsp. Cayenne Pepper | 0mg |
| ½ tsp. Onion Powder | 0mg |
| ½ tsp. Garlic Powder | 0mg |
| ¼ tsp. Thyme | 0mg |
| ⅛ tsp. Ground Clove | 0mg |
| ⅛ tsp. Nutmeg | 0mg |
| ⅛ tsp. All Spice | 0mg |

## How to:

Combine all ingredients in a small saucepan and simmer for 30 minutes.

**Suggestion:** Very good on chicken wings.

Yields: 2¼ cups (36 Tbsp.)
(1 serving = 1 Tbsp.)

## fyi:

**Brown Sugar:** For a healthier recipe, an equivalent brown sugar substitute may be substituted for brown sugar.

**Note:** Sodium content will change with amount of Hot Sauce.

Also, I prefer the Tobasco ® sauce brand for the hot sauce.

| Cal | Tot Fat | Sat Fat | Chol. | Potass | Carbs | Prot. | Fiber | Sugar |
|---|---|---|---|---|---|---|---|---|
| 32 | 1g | <1g | 3mg | 80mg | 6g | 0g | 0g | 2g |

CARB X-change ½

**Total Sodium** per serving
13mg

# Hot Wing Sauce

## Ingredients:

|  | Sodium per serving |
|---|---|
| ¾ cup Unsalted Butter | 1mg |
| ½ cup Hot Sauce, adjust to taste | 42mg |
| 2 tsp. Garlic Powder | 0mg |
| 1 tsp. Black Pepper | 0mg |

## How to:

Melt unsalted butter in a small bowl.

Add remaining ingredients and mix well.

Yields:  Approx. 20 servings
(1 serving = 1 Tbsp.)

## fyi:

**Note:**  Sodium content will change with amount of Hot Sauce.

Also, I prefer the Tobasco ® sauce brand for the hot sauce.

| Cal | Tot Fat | Sat Fat | Chol. | Potass | Carbs | Prot. | Fiber | Sugar |
|---|---|---|---|---|---|---|---|---|
| 62 | 7g | 4g | 19mg | 7mg | <1g | 0g | 0g | 0g |

CARB X-change 0

Total Sodium per serving
43mg

# Honey BBQ Sauce

## Ingredients:

| | Sodium per serving |
|---|---|
| ½ cup NSA Ketchup | 0mg |
| ⅓ cup Honey | <1mg |
| ¼ cup Light Corn Syrup | 5mg |
| 1 Tbsp. Cider Vinegar | 0mg |
| 1 tsp. Mustard Powder | 0mg |
| 1 tsp. Garlic Powder | <1mg |
| ½ tsp. Chili Powder | <1mg |
| ½ tsp. Onion Powder | 0mg |
| ¼ tsp. Cayenne Pepper, (optional or to taste) | 0mg |

## fyi:

**Chili Powder:** A no sodium chili powder is available in specialty stores or see recipe on page 5.

## How to:

Mix all ingredients in a small saucepan and simmer for 25 minutes.

Yields: Approx. 20 servings (1 serving = 1 Tbsp.)

| Cal | Tot Fat | Sat Fat | Chol. | Potass | Carbs | Prot. | Fiber | Sugar |
|---|---|---|---|---|---|---|---|---|
| 38 | 0g | 0g | 0mg | 11mg | 10g | <1g | <1g | 9g |

CARB X-change ½

Total Sodium per serving 6mg

# Pizza Sauce

## Ingredients:

| | Sodium per serving |
|---|---|
| 2 - 8 oz. cans of NSA Tomato Sauce | 4mg |
| 1 tsp. Sugar | 0mg |
| ½ tsp. Garlic Powder | 0mg |
| ¼ tsp. Thyme | 0mg |
| ¼ tsp. Oregano | 0mg |
| ¼ tsp. Basil | 0mg |
| ¼ tsp. Onion Powder | 0mg |
| ⅛ tsp. Black Pepper | 0mg |
| 1 Whole Bay Leaf | 0mg |
| 1 tsp. Lemon Juice | 0mg |

## How to:

Combine all ingredients in a small saucepan and simmer for 25 minutes.

Sauce is ready to use for pizza or other recipes.

Yields:  32 servings  (1 serving = 1 Tbsp.)

## fyi:

**Sugar:** For a healthier recipe, an equivalent sugar substitute may be substituted for sugar.

| Cal | Tot Fat | Sat Fat | Chol. | Potass | Carbs | Prot. | Fiber | Sugar |
|---|---|---|---|---|---|---|---|---|
| 5 | 0g | 0g | 0mg | 39mg | 1g | 0g | <1g | <1g |

CARB X-change 0

Total Sodium per serving
4mg

# Sweet BBQ Sauce

**On The** Stove:

## Ingredients:

| | Sodium per serving |
|---|---|
| 1½ cups NSA Ketchup | 0mg |
| 1 cup Brown Sugar, packed | <1mg |
| 6 oz. can Pineapple Juice | <1mg |
| ½ cup Red Wine Vinegar | 0mg |
| 1 Tbsp. Mustard Powder | 0mg |
| 1½ Tbsp. Worcestershire Sauce  | 5mg |
| 2 tsp. Paprika | 0mg |
| 2 tsp. Liquid Smoke | <1mg |
| 1 tsp. Garlic Powder | 0mg |
| 1 tsp. Black Pepper | 0mg |
| ½ tsp. Onion Powder | 0mg |
| ⅛ tsp. Cayenne Pepper, (optional) | 0mg |

## How to:

Combine all ingredients in a small saucepan and simmer for 20-25 minutes.

Yields: 48 servings (1 serving = 1 Tbsp.)

## fyi:

**Brown Sugar:** For a healthier recipe, an equivalent brown sugar substitute may be substituted for brown sugar.

| Cal | Tot Fat | Sat Fat | Chol. | Potass | Carbs | Prot. | Fiber | Sugar |
|---|---|---|---|---|---|---|---|---|
| 31 | 0g | 0g | 0mg | 27mg | 10g | 0g | <1g | 9g |

CARB X-change ½

Total Sodium per serving
7mg

it's in the **sauce**

# Chipotle BBQ Sauce

## Ingredients:

| | Sodium per serving |
|---|---|
| 1 Tbsp. Canola Oil | 0mg |
| ½ cup Onion, chopped | <1mg |
| ½ cup Bourbon | 0mg |
| 6 Garlic Cloves, finely minced | <1mg |
| 2 cups NSA Ketchup | 0mg |
| ⅓ cup Brown Sugar, packed | <1mg |
| ¼ cup Cider Vinegar | 0mg |
| ¼ cup Worcestershire Sauce | 12mg |
| 1½ Tbsp. Hickory Liquid Smoke | 1mg |
| 3 Chipotle Peppers in Adobo Sauce, (or to taste) | 8mg |
| ½ tsp. Thyme | 0mg |
| ¼ tsp. All Spice | 0mg |

## How to:

In a medium sauce pan, heat oil, and add garlic and onion.

Cook about 3-4 minutes on medium heat until onions are translucent.

Add bourbon and cook another 10 minutes.

Add remaining ingredients and simmer for 20 minutes.

Yields: 48 servings (1 serving = 1 Tbsp.)

---

### fyi:

**Chipotle Peppers:** For a lower sodium recipe, you may substitute ½ tsp. ground chipotle.

**Brown Sugar:** For a healthier recipe, an equivalent bown sugar substitute may be substituted for brown sugar.

| Cal | Tot Fat | Sat Fat | Chol. | Potass | Carbs | Prot. | Fiber | Sugar |
|---|---|---|---|---|---|---|---|---|
| 23 | <1g | 0g | 0mg | 11mg | 6g | 0g | 0g | 5g |

CARB X-change ½

Total Sodium per serving 22mg

# to
# begin
## with

# Easy Lime Shrimp

## Ingredients:

| | Sodium per serving |
|---|---|
| **1lb. Fresh Medium Size Shrimp,** peeled and deveined | 254mg |
| **1 Jalepeño,** seeded and finely minced | 0mg |
| **4 Tbsp. Unsalted Butter** | 0mg |
| **1 Tbsp. Cilantro,** minced | <1mg |
| **1 Lime,** juiced | <1mg |
| **2 Garlic Cloves,** minced | <1mg |

## How to:

Melt unsalted butter in a medium bowl and add jalepeño, cilantro, lime juice, and garlic cloves.

Place shrimp in a shallow baking dish, and pour butter mixture over shrimp.

Bake in oven for 10-15 minutes stirring shrimp a few times.

Yields: 4 servings (1 serving = 10-12 shrimp)

### fyi:
All ingredients can also be placed in foil packs and put on grill.

☑ FAMILY FAVORITE

| Cal | Tot Fat | Sat Fat | Chol. | Potass | Carbs | Prot. | Fiber | Sugar |
|---|---|---|---|---|---|---|---|---|
| 219 | 13g | 8g | 252mg | 234mg | 1g | 24g | <1g | <1g |

CARB X-change **0**

**Total Sodium** per serving
256mg

# Crispy Baked Chicken Strips

## Ingredients:

| Ingredient | Sodium per serving |
|---|---|
| 2 - 6 oz. Boneless, Skinless Chicken Breast  | 55mg |
| ½ cup Flour | <1mg |
| ½ tsp. Black Pepper | 0mg |
| 2 Large Eggs | 32mg |
| 1½ cup Plain Panko Bread Crumbs | 30mg |
| 1 tsp. Garlic Powder | 0mg |
| 1 tsp. Paprika | 0mg |
| ½ tsp. Cayenne Pepper, (optional) | 0mg |
| ½ tsp. Basil, dried | 0mg |
| ½ tsp. NSA Lemon Pepper Seasoning | 0mg |
| Non-Stick Cooking Spray | |

## How to:

Cut chicken into ½" strips.

Place flour and pepper in one shallow dish.

Place eggs in another, and mix bread crumbs, garlic powder, paprika, cayenne pepper, basil and lemon pepper on another dish.

Dip chicken in flour, and shake off excess.

Then dip in egg.

Finally dip in bread crumb mixture.

Place on baking sheet sprayed with cooking spray.

Place in oven for about 20 minutes or until done turning once.

For a crispier crust, finish chicken by broiling a couple of minutes each side in the oven.

Yields:  4 servings  (1 serving = 3 oz.)

## fyi:

**Frozen Chicken Breasts** will generally be higher in sodium than fresh.

Also, note that **fresh** and **frozen** chicken can be injected with sodium during the processing phase.

| Cal | Tot Fat | Sat Fat | Chol. | Potass | Carbs | Prot. | Fiber | Sugar |
|---|---|---|---|---|---|---|---|---|
| 274 | 4g | 1g | 156mg | 285mg | 31g | 27g | 1g | 2g |

Total Sodium per serving
117mg

# Chicken Wings

## Ingredients:

| | Sodium per serving |
|---|---|
| **1 pckg. (8) Chicken Wings** 🛒 | 23mg |
| **Non-Stick Cooking Spray** | |
| **A Sauce from this book** | |

(Jamaican Jerk, Hot Wing Sauce, or any of the BBQ Sauces)

## fyi:

**Frozen Chicken** will generally be higher in sodium than fresh.

Also, note that **fresh** and **frozen** chicken can be injected with sodium during the processing phase.

☑ FAMILY FAVORITE

## How to:

Boil wings in a large pot for 15 minutes.

Transfer to a broiler pan or baking sheet, and place in refrigerator for 30 minutes.

Cook wings for 45 minutes turning once.

Remove wings from oven and toss sauce over wings and place back on baking sheet or broiler pan.

Place back in oven 3-4 minutes or until sauce thickens.

Dip wings back in sauce for final coating.

Yields: 8 servings (1 serving = 1 wing)

➡Nutrition is figured without using Hot Wing Sauce on page 29.

| Cal | Tot Fat | Sat Fat | Chol. | Potass | Carbs | Prot. | Fiber | Sugar |
|---|---|---|---|---|---|---|---|---|
| 292 | 8g | 2g | 132mg | 450mg | 0g | 51g | 0g | 0g |

**CARB** X-change **0**

**Total Sodium** per serving 66mg

# Potato Skins

## Ingredients:

| | Sodium per serving |
|---|---|
| **6 Small to Medium Potatoes,** baked | 3mg |
| **¼ cup Olive Oil** | 0mg |
| **¼ tsp. Paprika** | <1mg |
| **¼ tsp. Black Pepper** | 0mg |
| **¼ tsp. Garlic Powder** | 0mg |
| **1 cup Shredded Cheddar Cheese** 🛒 | 58mg |
| **4 slices Low-Sodium Bacon** 🛒 | 33mg |
| **½ cup Light Sour Cream** 🛒 | 8mg |
| **4 Green Onions,** green part only, chopped | 0mg |
| **⅓ cup Tomatoes,** small dice | 1mg |

## How to:

Combine olive oil, paprika, pepper, and garlic powder in a small bowl.

Cut potatoes in half length-wise and allow to cool.

Scoop out flesh down to about ¼" and reserve for another use.

Brush both sides of potatoes with olive oil and place in roasting pan.

Bake in oven for 7 minutes on each side.

Remove and sprinkle cheese and bacon over the potatoes.

Place back in oven for 2 minutes.

Top the potatoes with green onions, tomatoes, and sour cream.

Yields: 12 servings (1 serving = 1 skin)

## fyi:

**Cheddar Cheese:** Shop and compare the cheeses that your supermarket carries. You may be able to find a low-sodium cheddar. Be aware that a 2% cheddar cheese may contain more sodium than a regular cheddar cheese.

| Cal | Tot Fat | Sat Fat | Chol. | Potass | Carbs | Prot. | Fiber | Sugar |
|---|---|---|---|---|---|---|---|---|
| 146 | 7g | 1g | 0mg | 536mg | 19g | 2g | 2g | 1g |

CARB X-change 2

**Total Sodium** per serving
104mg

# Chicken Tender Skewers

## Ingredients:

| | Sodium per serving |
|---|---|
| 20 Chicken Tenderloins 🛒 | 28mg |
| Wooden Skewers | |
| ½ cup Pineapple Juice | <1mg |
| 1½ Tbsp. Low Sodium 🛒 Teriyaki Sauce | 24mg |
| 1 Tbsp. Sesame Oil | 0mg |
| 1 tsp. Garlic Cloves, minced | <1mg |
| ¼ tsp. Ground Ginger | 0mg |
| 1½ Tbsp. Sesame Seeds | <1mg |

## fyi:

**Frozen Chicken** will generally be higher in sodium than fresh.

Also, note that **fresh** and **frozen** chicken can be injected with sodium during the processing phase.

## How to:

Place chicken in a large resealable plastic bag.

Mix remaining ingredients in a small bowl and pour into bag with chicken.

Marinate 6-8 hours.

Soak wooden skewers in water for 1-2hrs.

Thread chicken on skewers.

Grill.

**Suggestion:** Serve with sweet and sour sauce.

Yields: 20 servings (1 serving = 1 tenderloin)

| Cal | Tot Fat | Sat Fat | Chol. | Potass | Carbs | Prot. | Fiber | Sugar |
|---|---|---|---|---|---|---|---|---|
| 40 | 1g | <1g | 18mg | 12mg | 1g | 6g | <1g | 1g |

CARB X-change 0

Total Sodium 52mg per serving

# Fresh Salsa

**Just Mix:**

## Ingredients:

| | Sodium per serving |
|---|---|
| **4 medium Tomatoes,** chopped | 7mg |
| **1 Fresh Jalapeño,** minced <br> (Add more depending on your taste) | 0mg |
| **2 Limes,** juiced | 0mg |
| **1 medium Red Onion,** minced | <1mg |
| **1 bunch Fresh Cilantro,** chopped | 0mg |
| **½ cup NSA Ketchup** | 0mg |
| **1½ tsp. Garlic Powder** | <1mg |
| **1 tsp. Black Pepper** | 0mg |

## How to:

Combine all ingredients in a large bowl; mix well.

Let sit a few hours before serving.

Yields: 6 servings (1 serving = ½ cup)

| Cal | Tot Fat | Sat Fat | Chol. | Potass | Carbs | Prot. | Fiber | Sugar |
|---|---|---|---|---|---|---|---|---|
| 60 | <1g | 0g | 0mg | 243mg | 14g | 1g | 2g | 6g |

CARB X-change 1

Total Sodium per serving 9mg

# Guacamole

## Ingredients:

| | Sodium per serving |
|---|---|
| **3 Avacados,** peeled, pitted and mashed | 5mg |
| **2 Limes,** juiced | 4mg |
| **½ cup Red Onion,** minced | 0mg |
| **5 Tbsp. Fresh Cilantro,** chopped | 0mg |
| **2 Roma Tomatoes,** finely diced | 0mg |
| **2 Garlic Cloves,** minced | 0mg |
| **½ tsp. Cumin** | 0mg |
| **1 Jalepeño,** seeded, (optional) | 0mg |

## How to:

In a medium bowl, mix avocados and limes.

Mix in remaining ingredients.

Refrigerate for 1 hour.

Yields:  Approx. 16 servings  (1 serving = 1 Tbsp.)

| Cal | Tot Fat | Sat Fat | Chol. | Potass | Carbs | Prot. | Fiber | Sugar |
|---|---|---|---|---|---|---|---|---|
| 59 | 5g | <1g | 0mg | 25mg | 4g | <1g | 2g | <1g |

CARB X-change 0

Total Sodium per serving 9mg

# Grilled Onion Blossom

## Ingredients:

| | Sodium per serving |
|---|---|
| 1 Vidalia Onion | 2mg |
| 1 Tbsp. Unsalted Butter, melted | <1mg |
| 1 tsp. Sodium Free Chicken Flavor | 0mg |
| ½ tsp. Garlic Powder | 0mg |
| ½ tsp. Black Pepper | 0mg |
| Foil | |

## How to:

Cut the top off opposite the root end of the onion.

Peel back and cut away the first couple of layers.

Cut slits about a half an inch apart in the onion and spread apart the "pedals."

Place on a 12" x 12" sheet of aluminum foil.

Pour unsalted butter over the top of the onion and sprinkle spices over top.

Wrap up onion in foil and add another sheet of foil around it.

Grill for 20-30 minutes until onion is soft.

Yields: 2 servings  (1 serving = ½ onion)

| Cal | Tot Fat | Sat Fat | Chol. | Potass | Carbs | Prot. | Fiber | Sugar |
|---|---|---|---|---|---|---|---|---|
| 83 | 6g | 4g | 16mg | 134mg | 7g | 1g | 2g | <1g |

CARB X-change 0

Total Sodium per serving
3mg

# Fruit Dip

## Ingredients:

| | Sodium per serving |
|---|---|
| 1 - 8 oz. container of<br>**Fat Free Frozen Whipped Topping** | 7mg |
| 2 - 6 oz. containers of your<br>**favorite Yogurt** (I prefer a low-fat strawberry) | 9mg |

## How to:

Combine ingredients in a medium bowl.

Cover and place in refrigerator.

Yields:  18 servings  (1 serving = 1 Tbsp.)

✓ SUPER EASY

| Cal | Tot Fat | Sat Fat | Chol. | Potass | Carbs | Prot. | Fiber | Sugar |
|---|---|---|---|---|---|---|---|---|
| 32 | 0g | 0g | <1mg | 28mg | 6g | <1g | 0g | 3g |

CARB X-change 0

Total Sodium per serving 16mg

# Stuffed Mushrooms

Oven Temp: 375°F

## Ingredients:

| | Sodium per serving |
|---|---|
| **1 lb. Fresh Portabella Mushrooms,** (about 15 mushrooms) | 5mg |
| **3 Slices of Low Sodium Bacon**  | 57mg |
| **¼ cup Green Onion,** green part only | <1mg |
| **½ cup Fresh Mozzarella,** finely diced | 30mg |
| **½ cup Plain Panko Bread Crumbs** | 8mg |
| **1 Clove Garlic,** minced | 0mg |
| **½ tsp. Black Pepper,** minced | 0mg |

## fyi:

**Mozzarella:** Shop and compare the cheeses that your supermarket carries. You may be able to find a low-sodium cheddar. Be aware that a 2% cheddar cheese may contain more sodium than a regular cheddar cheese.

## How to:

Cut stems of mushrooms off and finely dice.

Place mushroom caps on a baking sheet.

Begin cooking bacon in a medium skillet.

When bacon is half way done add garlic and mushroom stems.

When bacon has finished cooking, remove from pan and finely dice.

Add bacon and remaining ingredients to pan and combine well.

Fill each of the mushroom caps with cheese mixture.

Bake in oven for 10-12 minutes until cheese melts.

Yields: 5 servings (1 serving = 3 pieces)

| Cal | Tot Fat | Sat Fat | Chol. | Potass | Carbs | Prot. | Fiber | Sugar |
|---|---|---|---|---|---|---|---|---|
| 121 | 6g | 3g | 17mg | 457mg | 10g | 8g | 2g | 2g |

 CARB X-change 0

 Total Sodium per serving 101mg

# Dill Vegetable Dip

Just Mix:

## Ingredients:

| | Sodium per serving |
|---|---|
| ¼ cup Light Mayonnaise | 19mg |
| ¾ cup Light Sour Cream | 9mg |
| 1½ Tbsp. Dry Dill Weed | 0mg |
| ¾ tsp. Garlic Powder | 0mg |
| ½ tsp. Oregano | 0mg |
| ⅛ tsp. Ground Sage | 0mg |

## How to:

Mix all ingredients in a small bowl. Serve

Yields: 16 servings (1 serving = 1 Tbsp.)

☑ SUPER EASY

| Cal | Tot Fat | Sat Fat | Chol. | Potass | Carbs | Prot. | Fiber | Sugar |
|---|---|---|---|---|---|---|---|---|
| 25 | 2g | 1g | 4mg | 11mg | 2g | 1g | 0g | 1g |

CARB X-change **0**

Total Sodium per serving
28mg

# the
# main
## dish

# Chicken Pot Pie

**Oven Temp:**
400°F

## Ingredients:

| | Sodium per serving |
|---|---|
| 2 Tbsp. Canola Oil | 0mg |
| 4 cups of Frozen Mixed Vegetables 🛒 | 30mg |
| 3 Tbsp. Unsalted Butter | <1mg |
| 1 cup Onion, chopped | <1mg |
| 1 cup Celery, chopped | 13mg |
| 2 Garlic Cloves, minced | <1mg |
| 1½ cups 50% less Sodium 🛒 Chicken Broth | 84mg |
| ½ cup Skim Milk | 5mg |
| 3 Tbsp. Flour | <1mg |
| ½ tsp. Sage | 0mg |
| ¼ tsp. Thyme | 0mg |
| ½ tsp. Garlic Powder | <1mg |
| 1 Tbsp. Dried Parsley Flakes | <1mg |
| ½ tsp. Black Pepper | 0mg |
| 2 cups Chicken, cooked and shredded 🛒 | 38mg |

## Crust:

| | |
|---|---|
| 1 cup All-Purpose Flour | 0mg |
| ⅓ cup Skim Milk | 5mg |
| 2 tsp. Baking Powder 🛒 | 13mg |
| ¼ cup Unsalted Butter, chilled | 1mg |

## fyi:

**Frozen Chicken Breasts** will generally be higher in sodium than fresh.

Also, note that **fresh** and **frozen** chicken can be injected with sodium during the processing phase.

**Chicken Broth:** For an even lower sodium recipe, use recipe on page 27.

## How to:

Make crust ahead of time by combining crust ingredients, wrap tightly in plastic wrap, and then place in refrigerator for at least an hour before baking.

Toss mixed vegetables with canola oil and place on baking sheet.

Place in oven and roast 10-15 minutes.

In a large skillet, melt unsalted butter and add celery, onion, and garlic. Cook for 5-6 minutes or until tender.

In a small saucepan heat chicken broth and milk.

When onion mixture is tender, mix in flour, sage, thyme, garlic powder, parsley and black pepper. Add broth and milk mixture and heat and stir until sauce thickens.
.

Add cooked chicken and vegetables to skillet, and mix well.

Place filling into 2½ qt. casserole dish.

Roll crust and place on top of filling.

Lower the temperature of the oven to 350°F and cook 30-35 minutes.

Yields: 8 servings (1 serving - Approx. 1 cup)

| Cal | Tot Fat | Sat Fat | Chol. | Potass | Carbs | Prot. | Fiber | Sugar |
|---|---|---|---|---|---|---|---|---|
| 360 | 15g | 7g | 62mg | 418mg | 36g | 20g | 4g | 6g |

CARB X-change 2½

Total Sodium per serving 174mg

# Baked Chicken Parmesean

## Ingredients:

| | Sodium per serving |
|---|---|
| **4-6 oz. Boneless Skinless**  **Chicken Breast** | 111mg |
| **1⅓ Cup Tomato Sauce or** (For lower sodium see recipe on page 28.) | 32mg |
| **2 Large Eggs** | 32mg |
| **1 Cup Flour** | <1mg |
| **2 cups Plain Panko Bread Crumbs**  | 40mg |
| **1 Tbsp. Dried Parsley** | 1mg |
| **1 tsp. Dried Basil** | <1mg |
| **½ tsp. Dried Oregano** | 0mg |
| **½ tsp. Black Pepper** | 0mg |
| **¼ cup Parmesan Cheese**  | 116mg |
| **4 oz. Fresh Mozzarella Cheese**  | 25mg |
| **1 pkg. (16 oz.) Fettuccini** (Follow package directions - minus the salt) | 1mg |

## fyi:

For a faster recipe, substitute a low sodium jar of spaghetti sauce.

**Frozen Chicken Breasts** will generally be higher in sodium than fresh.

Also, note that **fresh** and **frozen** chicken can be injected with sodium during the processing phase.

**Fresh Mozzarella** contains less sodium than shredded and packaged Mozzarella.

## How to:

Place chicken in-between 2 pieces of plastic wrap and flatten to about ½ ".

Place flour in a shallow bowl,

Place egg in small bowl and beat.

Place bread crumbs, parsley, basil, oregano, and pepper in another small bowl.

Dip chicken in flour, and shake off any excess. Then dip chicken in egg.

Finally dip in bread crumb mixture and place on baking sheet and let sit 5 minutes.

Place in oven, and bake for 20-25 minutes turning once. An internal temperature of 165°F is recommended.

When chicken is finished, top with ⅓ cup of tomato sauce, 1 Tbsp. of parmesan cheese, and 1 oz. mozzarella cheese. Place back in oven for 5-10 minutes until cheese melts.

Serve on a 4 oz. bed of fettuccine noodles (or what you have on hand).

Yields:  4 servings  (1 serving = 1 chicken breast)

| Cal | Tot Fat | Sat Fat | Chol. | Potass | Carbs | Prot. | Fiber | Sugar |
|---|---|---|---|---|---|---|---|---|
| 996 | 16g | 6g | 289mg | 735mg | 141g | 67g | 6g | 7g |

CARB X-change 4

Total Sodium per serving
358mg

# Chicken Teriyaki Stir-Fry with Vegetables

## Ingredients:

| | Sodium per serving |
|---|---|
| 2 Tbsp. Cornstarch | 0mg |
| ½ cup Low-Sodium Chicken Broth | 56mg |
| 2 Tbsp. Low-Sodium Teriyaki Sauce | 160mg |
| ¼ cup Light Corn Syrup | 25mg |
| 4 Tbsp. Extra Virgin Olive Oil, divided | 0mg |
| 2 Garlic Cloves, minced | <1mg |
| 4 cups Fresh Vegetables | 26mg |

(Mushrooms, Green Pepper, Snow Peas, Water Chestnuts, Broccoli, Celery, Carrots, Red Bell Pepper, or Bean Sprouts.)

| | |
|---|---|
| 10 oz. Boneless, Skinless Chicken Breast | 55mg |

## How to:

In a small bowl combine cornstarch, broth, teriyaki sauce, and corn syrup.

In a large skillet or wok, heat 2 Tbsp. oil on high.

Add garlic and vegetables. Stir fry quickly until vegetables are tender.

Remove vegetables from skillet or wok.

Add 2 Tbsp. oil and cook chicken until done.

Pour vegetables back in skillet or wok and add sauce. Bring to a boil, stirring often.

Cook until sauce thickens.

**Suggestion:** Serve with Rice.

Yields: 4 servings

## fyi:

**Chicken Breasts** can be substituted for a whole chicken. Frozen Chicken Breasts will generally be higher in Sodium than fresh.

Also, note that **fresh** and **frozen** chicken can be injected with sodium during the processing phase.

**Chicken Broth:** For an even lower sodium recipe use recipe on page 27.

→Nutrition is figured without rice

| Cal | Tot Fat | Sat Fat | Chol. | Potass | Carbs | Prot. | Fiber | Sugar |
|---|---|---|---|---|---|---|---|---|
| 342 | 15g | 2g | 49mg | 476mg | 30g | 22g | 2g | 21g |

CARB X-change 2

Total Sodium per serving 322mg

# Chicken with Pasta

## Ingredients:

| | Sodium per serving |
|---|---|
| ¼ cup Sun-Dried Tomatoes,  chopped, (Not packed in oil) | 71mg |
| 4 - 6 oz. Boneless, Skinless Chicken Breast | 74mg |
| 1 Tbsp. Extra Virgin Olive Oil | 0mg |
| 1 tsp. Basil | 0mg |
| ¼ tsp. Garlic Powder | 0mg |
| 3 Tbsp. White Wine Vinegar | 0mg |
| 3 cups uncooked Penne Pasta | 4mg |
| ⅓ cup Green Bell Pepper, finely chopped | 0mg |
| 2 Tbsp. Parmesan Cheese, grated | 47mg |

## fyi:

**Pasta:** Find pasta with more nutritional benefits like whole grain and high fiber.

**Frozen Chicken Breasts** will generally be higher in sodium than fresh.

Also, note that **fresh** and **frozen** chicken can be injected with sodium during the processing phase.

## How to:

Soak tomatoes in hot water for 10-15 minutes.

Chop chicken into small pieces and saute' in large skillet with olive oil.

Cook pasta according to package directions, minus the salt, if it calls for any.

Drain tomatoes and add basil, garlic powder, and vinegar.

Add green pepper in with chicken.

Combine pasta, chicken mixture, and tomato mixture.

Top with parmesan cheese.

Yields:  4 servings
(1 serving = 1 chicken breast)

| Cal | Tot Fat | Sat Fat | Chol. | Potass | Carbs | Prot. | Fiber | Sugar |
|---|---|---|---|---|---|---|---|---|
| 190 | 4g | 1g | 2mg | 122mg | 35g | 6g | 5g | 2g |

Total Sodium per serving
196mg

# Margarita Chicken

## Ingredients:

| | Sodium per serving |
|---|---|
| 4- 6 oz. Boneless, Skinless Chicken Breast  | 111mg |
| 1- can of Frozen Margarita Mix | 0mg |
| ¼ cup Fresh Cilantro | 0mg |
| ½ tsp. Cumin | 0mg |

**fyi**⁚

**Frozen Chicken Breasts** will generally be higher in sodium than fresh.

Also, note that **fresh** and **frozen** chicken can be injected with sodium during the processing phase.

## How to:

Combine all ingredients in a small resealable bag.

Let marinate for 6-8 hours.

Grill on low heat. An internal temperature of 165°F is recommended.

**Suggestion:** Serve over rice.

Yields: 4 servings
(1 serving = 1 - 6 oz. chicken breast)

→Nutrition is figured without rice

| Cal | Tot Fat | Sat Fat | Chol. | Potass | Carbs | Prot. | Fiber | Sugar |
|---|---|---|---|---|---|---|---|---|
| 278 | 2g | <1g | 99mg | 443mg | 25g | 39g | 0g | 23g |

CARB X-change 2

Total Sodium per serving 111mg

# Chicken Salad

## Ingredients:

| | Sodium per serving |
|---|---|
| 3 cups Boneless, Skinless Chicken Breast | 73mg |
| 5 Tbsp. Light Mayonnaise | 50mg |
| 5 Tbsp. Light Sour Cream | 10mg |
| 2 Tbsp. Celery, finely chopped | 3mg |
| 2 Tbsp. Cucumber | 0mg |
| 2 Tbsp. Green Onion, finely chopped | 0mg |
| ½ tsp. Garlic Powder | 0mg |
| ¼ tsp. Basil | 0mg |

## How to:

Boil chicken in sauce pan until done.

Dice or shred chicken.

Combine with all other ingredients in a small bowl and mix well.

Yields:  6 servings  (1 serving = ½ cup)

## fyi:

**Pasta:** Find pasta with more nutritional benefits like whole grain and high fiber.

**Frozen Chicken Breasts** will generally be higher in sodium than fresh.

Also, note that **fresh** and **frozen** chicken can be injected with sodium during the processing phase.

**Mayonnaise:** I have found the store brand is generally lower in sodium.

| Cal | Tot Fat | Sat Fat | Chol. | Potass | Carbs | Prot. | Fiber | Sugar |
|---|---|---|---|---|---|---|---|---|
| 172 | 5g | 7g | 70mg | 306mg | 2g | 27g | <1g | <1g |

CARB X-change 0

Total Sodium per serving 136mg

# Chicken Cacciatore

## Ingredients:

| | Sodium per serving |
|---|---|
| 1 Whole Chicken (3-4 lbs.)  | 137mg |
| cut into pieces, skin removed | |
| Flour for dredging | 0mg |
| 3 Tbsp. Olive Oil | 0mg |
| ¼ cup Onion, chopped | <1mg |
| 2 Garlic Cloves, minced | <1mg |
| 1 - 6 oz. can of NSA Tomato Paste | 26mg |
| ¾ cup Lower Sodium Chicken Broth or Stock | 84mg |
| ½ cup White Wine | 2mg |
| ½ tsp. Basil | 0mg |
| ¼ tsp. Black Pepper | 0mg |
| 1 Bay Leaf | 0mg |
| ¼ tsp. Rosemary, dried | 0mg |
| ¼ tsp. Thyme | 0mg |
| 1½ cups Fresh Portabella Mushrooms | <1mg |
| 1 Green Pepper, thinly sliced | <1mg |

## How to:

Coat chicken with flour.

In a large deep skillet or pot, saute´ chicken with olive oil until browned.

Add onions and garlic. Saute´ a couple more minutes.

Remove the chicken from the pan and add the remaining ingredients.

Mix well and add chicken back to pot and simmer, covered on low heat for 45 minutes - 1 hour until chicken is done. An internal temperature of 165°F is recommended.

**Suggestion:** Serve with rice.

Yields: 4 servings (1 serving = ¼ of chicken)

## fyi:

**Chicken Breasts** can be substituted for a whole chicken. Frozen chicken breasts will generally be higher in sodium than fresh.

**Frozen Chicken Breasts** will generally be higher in sodium than fresh.

Also, note that **fresh** and **frozen** chicken can be injected with sodium during the processing phase.

**Chicken Broth:** For an even lower sodium recipe, use recipe on page 27.

→Nutrition is figured without rice

| Cal | Tot Fat | Sat Fat | Chol. | Potass | Carbs | Prot. | Fiber | Sugar |
|---|---|---|---|---|---|---|---|---|
| 386 | 15g | 3g | 119mg | 611mg | 15g | 41g | 5g | 8g |

CARB X-change 1

Total Sodium per serving
251mg

# Oven Fried Chicken

**Oven Temp:**
425°F

## Ingredients:

| | Sodium per serving |
|---|---|
| **1 Whole Chicken (3-4 lbs.),** <br>cut into pieces, skin removed | 137mg |
| **½ cup Light Mayonnaise** | 120mg |
| **¼ cup Skim Milk** | 15mg |
| **2 cups Plain Panko Bread Crumbs** | 40mg |
| **⅓ cup Fresh Parsley** | 3mg |
| **3 Tbsp. Extra Virgin Olive Oil** | 0mg |
| **1½ tsp. Garlic Powder** | 0mg |
| **1 tsp. Paprika** | 0mg |
| **½ tsp. Onion Powder** | 0mg |
| **½ tsp. Black Pepper** | 0mg |
| **¼ tsp. Cayenne Pepper,** (optional) | 0mg |

## fyi:

**Chicken Breasts** can be substituted for a whole chicken. Frozen chicken breasts will generally be higher in sodium than fresh.

**Frozen Chicken Breasts** will generally be higher in sodium than fresh.

Also, note that **fresh** and **frozen** chicken can be injected with sodium during the processing phase.

**Mayonnaise:** I have found the store brand is generally lower in sodium.

## How to:

Place chicken in a large plastic storage bag.

Whisk together mayonnaise and milk in a medium bowl. Pour into bag with chicken and toss to coat. This can sit for a few hours in the refrigerator before baking.

In another bowl combine bread crumbs, parsley, olive oil, garlic powder, onion powder, black pepper, paprika, and cayenne pepper.

Take chicken pieces out of bag one at a time and dip into the bread crumb mixture and place in a large greased baking dish.

Bake in oven, uncovered, for 45 to 55 minutes or until Chicken is no longer pink.

Breast - An internal temperature of 165°F is recommended.

Thighs and drumsticks - An internal temperature of 180°F is recommended.

Yields: 4 servings
(1 serving = 1 breast or 1 large quarter)

| Cal | Tot Fat | Sat Fat | Chol. | Potass | Carbs | Prot. | Fiber | Sugar |
|---|---|---|---|---|---|---|---|---|
| 492 | 23g | 4g | 120mg | 545mg | 29g | 42g | 7g | 3g |

CARB X-change 2

Total Sodium per serving
312mg

# Chicken Tettrazini

## Ingredients:

| | Sodium per serving |
|---|---|
| 8 oz. Thin Spaghetti | 17mg |
| 4 Tbsp. Unsalted Butter, divided | 1mg |
| 2 - 6oz. Boneless, Skinless Chicken Breast | 37mg |
| 1½ cups Portabella Mushrooms, sliced | <1mg |
| 1 cup Onions, chopped | <1mg |
| 2 Garlic Cloves, minced | 0mg |
| ½ cup White Wine | 1mg |
| 2 Tbsp. Fresh Flat Leaf Parsley | 0mg |
| ½ cup Frozen Peas | 13mg |
| 3 Tbsp. Flour | 0mg |
| 1 cup Skim Milk | 20mg |
| 1½ cup Low Sodium Chicken Broth or Stock | 112mg |
| ¼ tsp. Black Pepper | 0mg |
| A Pinch of Nutmeg | 0mg |
| ½ cup Parmesan Cheese, divided | 170mg |
| ½ cup Plain Panko Bread Crumbs | 7mg |

## fyi:

**Chicken Broth:** For an even lower sodium recipe, use recipe on page 27.

**Frozen Chicken Breasts** will generally be higher in sodium than fresh.

Also, note that **fresh** and **frozen** chicken can be injected with sodium during the processing phase.

## How to:

Cook spaghetti according to package directions (minus the salt). Drain.

Add 1 Tbsp. unsalted butter to a large skillet and saute' chicken until done. Remove chicken from pan.

Add onion, mushrooms, and garlic to pan and saute' for a couple minutes until onions start to soften.

Add white wine to onions, cook for 2-3 minutes, and add onion mixture, parsley, and peas into bowl with chicken.

In skillet, melt remaining butter. Slowly whisk in flour, milk, and chicken broth.

Next, add pepper, nutmeg, and ¼ cup parmesan cheese and continue stirring until sauce thickens.

Add cooked spaghetti to chicken and mix well. Spray a 9"x 13" baking dish with non-stick spray and add chicken mixture to dish.

Slowly pour sauce over spaghetti and "push" sauce down into spaghetti. Mix remaining parmesan and bread crumbs, and sprinkle over spaghetti.

Bake for 30 minutes or until bubbly.

Yields: 6 servings  (1 serving = Approx. 1 cup)

| Cal | Tot Fat | Sat Fat | Chol. | Potass | Carbs | Prot. | Fiber | Sugar |
|---|---|---|---|---|---|---|---|---|
| 391 | 12g | 7g | 54mg | 362mg | 40g | 28g | 4g | 2g |

CARB X-change 2½

Total Sodium per serving
382mg

# Chicken Marsala

## Ingredients:

| | Sodium per serving |
|---|---|
| 4 - 6 oz. Boneless, Skinless  Chicken Breast | 111mg |
| ¼ cup Flour | <1mg |
| ½ tsp. Black Pepper | 0mg |
| ½ tsp. Oregano | 0mg |
| 2 Tbsp. Olive Oil | 0mg |
| 2 Tbsp. Unsalted Butter, divided | <1mg |
| 1½ cups Mushrooms, Use your favorite | 1mg |
| ¼ cup Onion, diced | <1mg |
| 2 Garlic Cloves, minced | <1mg |
| ½ cup Marsala Wine | 190mg |
| ½ cup Low Sodium Chicken Broth | 56mg |
| ¼ cup Fresh Flat Leaf Parsley | 2mg |

## fyi:

**Chicken Broth:** For an even lower sodium recipe, use recipe on page 27.

**Frozen Chicken Breasts** will generally be higher in sodium than fresh.

Also, note that **fresh** and **frozen** chicken can be injected with sodium during the processing phase.

## How to:

Heat olive oil and 1 Tbsp. unsalted butter in a large skillet over medium high heat.

In a shallow dish, add flour, pepper, and oregano. Dredge each piece of chicken in flour mixture and place in hot skillet.

Brown each side for 5-6 minutes.

Remove chicken from pan and add the other Tbsp. of butter with the mushrooms, onions, and garlic. Cook over medium heat 2-3 minutes until onions turn slightly brown.

Add Marsala Wine and continue to cook 2-3 minutes.

Stir in chicken broth and return chicken to pan. Cover and finish cooking until chicken reaches an internal temperature of 165°F.

When chicken is finished, sprinkle parsley on top.

**Suggestion:** Serve with your favorite pasta, rice, or even couscous.

Yields: 4 servings
(1 serving = 1 chicken breast)

→Nutrition is figured without pasta, rice, or couscous

| Cal | Tot Fat | Sat Fat | Chol. | Potass | Carbs | Prot. | Fiber | Sugar |
|---|---|---|---|---|---|---|---|---|
| 366 | 15g | 5g | 114mg | 362mg | 12g | 45g | 1g | <1g |

CARB X-change 1

Total Sodium per serving
362mg

# Slow Cooker Chicken

## Ingredients:

| | Sodium per serving |
|---|---|
| Foil | |
| **1 Whole Chicken (3 - 4 lbs.)**, washed | 157mg |
| **Non-Stick Olive Oil Spray** | <1mg |
| **1 tsp. Black Pepper** | 0mg |
| **2 Carrots,** roughly chopped | 25mg |
| **2 Celery Stalks with Leaves,** roughly chopped | 28mg |
| **1 Small Onion,** roughly chopped | <1mg |
| **5 Garlic Cloves,** peeled and smashed | <1mg |
| **½ cup Fresh Parsley,** chopped | 4mg |

## fyi:

**Frozen Chicken Breasts** will generally be higher in sodium than fresh.

Also, note that **fresh** and **frozen** chicken can be injected with sodium during the processing phase.

☑ SUPER EASY

## How to:

Tear 6-7 sheets of foil 12-16" long and form into loose balls (about baseball size).

Place the foil balls in the bottom of the slow cooker.

Spray chicken with olive oil spray and dust with black pepper.

Add a few pieces of the carrots, celery, onion, and 2 garlic cloves into cavity of chicken.

Place chicken in slow cooker.

Scatter remaining carrots, celery, and onion in bottom of slow cooker.

Sprinkle parsley over chicken and cover.

Cook for 8 hours on low setting.

**For Optional Gravy:**
When finished pour juices into small bowl and skim fat off the top. (See recipe on page 22.)

Yields: 4 servings
(1 serving = 1 breast or 1 large quarter)

| Cal | Tot Fat | Sat Fat | Chol. | Potass | Carbs | Prot. | Fiber | Sugar |
|---|---|---|---|---|---|---|---|---|
| 260 | 6g | 1g | 136mg | 739mg | 7g | 43g | 2g | 2g |

CARB X-change ½

Total Sodium 210mg per serving

# Stuffed Chicken Breast

## Ingredients:

| | Sodium per serving |
|---|---|
| 1 cup Boiling Water | 0mg |
| ¼ cup Sun-Dried Tomatoes,  packed without oil | 71mg |
| 3 Tbsp. Olive Oil, divided | 0mg |
| ¼ cup Red Onion | <1mg |
| ¼ cup Frozen Artichoke Hearts, chopped | 4mg |
| 1 Garlic Clove, minced | <1mg |
| 2 oz. Goat Cheese | 52mg |
| 1 tsp. Basil, divided | 0mg |
| 1 tsp. Thyme, divided | 0mg |
| ⅛ tsp. Black Pepper | 0mg |
| 4 - 6 oz. Boneless, Skinless Chicken Breast | 111mg |
| 1 cup Low-Sodium Chicken Broth | 112mg |
| 2 tsp. Cornstarch | 0mg |
| 2 Tbsp. Lemon Juice | 0mg |

### fyi:

Frozen Chicken Breasts will generally be higher in sodium than fresh.

Also, note that **fresh** and **frozen** chicken can be injected with sodium during the processing phase.

**Chicken Broth:** For an even lower sodium recipe use recipe on page 27.

## How to:

Add tomatoes to boiling water and let stand for 15-20 minutes.

Heat 1 Tbsp. olive oil in a large skillet and add red onion, artichoke hearts, and garlic.
Heat for 4-5 minutes.

Place in bowl and add ½ of the basil and thyme, and all of the black pepper, tomatoes, and goat cheese.

Cut a small 1" slit into the thickest part of the chicken and stuff with about 2 Tbsp. of cheese mixture.

Heat other 2 Tbsp. of olive oil in pan and add chicken. Cook each side about 8 minutes.

Remove from pan, cover, and keep chicken warm.

Bring chicken broth, lemon juice, cornstarch, remaining basil, and thyme to a boil.

Stir until sauce thickens.

Add chicken back to pan, cover, and cook an additional 5 minutes or until an internal temperature of 165°F is reached.

Serve sauce over chicken.

Yields: 4 servings
(1 serving = 1 chicken breast)

| Cal | Tot Fat | Sat Fat | Chol. | Potass | Carbs | Prot. | Fiber | Sugar |
|---|---|---|---|---|---|---|---|---|
| 271 | 8g | 3g | 105mg | 592mg | 6g | 43g | 1g | 2g |

CARB X-change ½

Total Sodium per serving
351mg

# Simple, Simple Chicken

## Ingredients:

|  | Sodium per serving |
|---|---|
| **4 - 6 oz. Boneless, Skinless**  **Chicken Breast** | 110mg |
| **2 Tbsp. Italian Dressing Mix** ( See recipe on page 6.) | 1mg |
| **2 Tbsp. Water** | 0mg |
| **1 tsp. Lemon Juice** | 0mg |
| **⅔ cup Canola Oil** | 0mg |
| **1-2 tsp. Red Pepper Flakes,** optional | 0mg |

## How to:

Mix all ingredients except chicken in a small bowl, jar, or food processor.

Place chicken in a large resealable bag and add Italian dressing mixture.

Let marinate in refrigerator for 4-6 hours.

Cook on grill or place in a covered dish in oven until an internal temperature of 165°F is reached.

Yields:  4 servings  (1 serving = 1 chicken breast)

### fyi:

Frozen Chicken Breasts will generally be higher in sodium than fresh.

Also, note that **fresh** and **frozen** chicken can be injected with sodium during the processing phase.

| Cal | Tot Fat | Sat Fat | Chol. | Potass | Carbs | Prot. | Fiber | Sugar |
|---|---|---|---|---|---|---|---|---|
| 508 | 38g | 3g | 99mg | 435mg | 1g | 39g | 0g | 0g |

CARB X-change 0

Total Sodium per serving
111mg

# Grilled Honey-Balsamic Chicken

## Ingredients:

| | Sodium per serving |
|---|---|
| 4 - 6 oz. Boneless, Skinless  Chicken Breast | 111mg |
| 4 Tbsp. Honey | <1mg |
| 2 Tbsp. Balsamic Vinegar | 3mg |
| 2 tsp. Olive Oil | 0mg |
| 2 Tbsp. Lemon Juice | 0mg |
| 1 tsp. Garlic Herb Seasoning, (ex. Mrs. Dash) | 0mg |

## How to:

Combine honey, vinegar, olive oil, lemon juice, and seasoning in a small bowl.

Reserve 2-3 Tbsp. of liquid in a small bowl and refrigerate.

Place chicken and remaining marinade in a medium storage bag and refrigerate for at least 2 hours.

Cook chicken on grill until done.

Pour reserved liquid on chicken a couple of minutes before taking off grill.

Yields: 4 servings
(1 serving = 1 chicken breast)

### fyi:

**Frozen Chicken Breasts** will generally be higher in sodium than fresh.

Also, note that **fresh** and **frozen** chicken can be injected with sodium during the processing phase.

| Cal | Tot Fat | Sat Fat | Chol. | Potass | Carbs | Prot. | Fiber | Sugar |
|---|---|---|---|---|---|---|---|---|
| 317 | 9g | 2g | 99mg | 464mg | 19g | 39g | <1g | 18g |

**CARB** X-change **1**

**Total Sodium** per serving
114mg

# Hawaiian Chicken

## Ingredients:

| Ingredient | Sodium per serving |
|---|---|
| 4 - 6 oz. Boneless, Skinless Chicken Breast | 111mg |
| 2 Tbsp. Low Sodium Teriyaki Sauce | 160mg |
| 2 Tbsp. Brown Sugar, packed | 3mg |
| 1 Tbsp. Sesame Oil | 0mg |
| 1½ Tbsp. White Wine Vinegar | 0mg |
| ¼ tsp. Ground Ginger | 0mg |
| ¼ tsp. Garlic Powder (From Can of Pineapple ) | 0mg |
| 3 Tbsp. Pineapple Juice, | 4mg |
| 1 - 8 oz. can Pineapple Rings | 10mg |

### fyi:

**Frozen Chicken Breasts** will generally be higher in sodium than fresh.

Also, note that **fresh** and **frozen** chicken can be injected with sodium during the processing phase.

**Brown Sugar:** For a healthier recipe, an equivalent brown sugar substitute may be substituted for brown sugar.

☑ SUPER EASY

## How to:

Combine all the ingredients in a resealable bag except pineapple rings, and marinate for 3-4 hours in the refrigerator.

Grill chicken until reaching an internal temperature of 160°F.

Grill pineapple 2-3 minutes on each side and serve on top of chicken.

Yields:  4 servings  (1 serving = 1 chicken breast)

| Cal | Tot Fat | Sat Fat | Chol. | Potass | Carbs | Prot. | Fiber | Sugar |
|---|---|---|---|---|---|---|---|---|
| 319 | 6g | 1g | 99mg | 477mg | 26g | 40g | 1g | 25g |

CARB X-change 2

Total Sodium per serving 288mg

# Chicken Burgers

## Ingredients:

| | Sodium per serving |
|---|---|
| 1½ lbs. Ground Chicken, (or put equal amount of whole chicken breasts in food processor) | 135mg |
| ⅓ cup Red Bell Pepper, finely chopped | <1mg |
| ⅓ cup Tomatoes, seeded and finely chopped (Roma tomatoes are delicious) | 1mg |
| ⅓ cup Fresh Mushrooms, finely chopped | 0mg |
| 1 Medium Carrot, shredded | 12mg |
| ⅓ cup Onions, finely chopped | <1mg |
| ½ cup Panko Bread Crumbs | 10mg |
| 1 Large Egg | 16mg |
| 1 Garlic Clove, finely chopped | 0mg |
| Peppercorn Medley, (few turns of medley grinder) | 0mg |
| 4 Hamburger Buns | 206mg |

## How to:

Combine all ingredients except buns in a medium bowl.

Divide into 4 equal parts and form into patties.

Grill.

An internal temperature of 165°F is recommended.

Yields:  4 servings  (1 serving = 1 burger)

## fyi:

**Frozen Chicken Breasts** will generally be higher in sodium than fresh.

Also, note that **fresh** and **frozen** chicken can be injected with sodium during the processing phase.

| Cal | Tot Fat | Sat Fat | Chol. | Potass | Carbs | Prot. | Fiber | Sugar |
|---|---|---|---|---|---|---|---|---|
| 488 | 21g | 5g | 196mg | 188mg | 34g | 39g | 2g | 5g |

CARB X-change 2

Total Sodium per serving
382mg

# BBQ Chicken Loaf

**Oven Temp:**
400°F

## Ingredients:

| | Sodium per serving |
|---|---|
| 1½ lbs. Ground Chicken, 🛒 (or put equal amount of whole chicken breasts in food processor) | 135mg |
| ½ cup Red Bell Peper, finely chopped | <1mg |
| ½ Red Onions, finely chopped | 1mg |
| ¾ cup Plain Panko Bread Crumbs 🛒 | 0mg |
| 1 Large Egg | 12mg |
| ⅔ cup BBQ Sauce, divided 🛒 | <1mg |
| ½ cup Cheddar Cheese 🛒 | 10mg |

## How to:

Combine ⅓ cup BBQ sauce and remaining ingredients in a large bowl and press into a 10" x 6" loaf pan.

Bake for 40-45 minutes

An internal temperature of 165°F is recommended. Once done, top loaf with remaining BBQ sauce.

Slice into 8 equal slices.

Yields: 8 servings (1 serving = 1 slice)

---

### fyi:

**Cheddar Cheese:** Shop and compare the cheeses that your supermarket carries. You may be able to find a low-sodium cheddar. Be aware that a 2% cheddar cheese may contain more sodium than a regular cheddar cheese.

**BBQ Sauce:** I use the Honey BBQ sauce in this book on page 31 for this recipe.

| Cal | Tot Fat | Sat Fat | Chol. | Potass | Carbs | Prot. | Fiber | Sugar |
|---|---|---|---|---|---|---|---|---|
| 208 | 4g | 2g | 83mg | 262mg | 19g | 23g | <1g | 13g |

CARB X-change 1

Total Sodium per serving
158mg

# Fajitas

## Ingredients:

| | Beef Sodium per serving | Chicken Sodium per serving |
|---|---|---|
| ¼ cup Orange Juice | | <1mg |
| ⅓ cup Fresh Lime Juice | | <1mg |
| ¼ cup Olive Oil | | 0mg |
| 3 Garlic Cloves, minced | | <1mg |
| 1 Jalapeño, seeded and minced | | 0mg |
| 3 Tbsp. Cilantro Leaves, chopped | | 0mg |
| 1 tsp. Cumin | | <1mg |
| ¼ tsp. Black Pepper | | 0mg |
| ¼ tsp. Onion Powder | | 0mg |
| 2 lbs. Chicken Breast  or Flank Steak (may mix meats) | 110mg | 98mg |
| Juice from 1 Lime | | 0mg |
| 1½ Tbsp. Extra Virgin Olive Oil | | 0mg |
| 1 Large Onion, Sliced into strips | | <1mg |
| 2 Large Green Peppers, Sliced into Strips | | 0mg |
| 12 Medium Flour Tortillas | | 305mg |
| ½ cup Light Sour Cream (optional) | | 17mg |

## How to:

Combine the first 9 ingredients in a small bowl and pour into a resealable bag.

Slice steak or chicken into thin strips and add to marinade in bag.

Place in refrigerator for 4-6 hours.

In a large bowl, add the sliced onion and green pepper.

Pour olive oil and juice from one lime over meat, onions, and green peppers and toss.

Grill steak, chicken, onion, and green pepper until done.

Top with sour cream, if desired.

Yields: 6 servings
(1 serving = 2 dressed tortillas per serving)

## fyi:

**Frozen Chicken Breasts** will generally be higher in sodium than fresh.

Also, note that **fresh** and **frozen** chicken can be injected with sodium during the processing phase.

→Nutritional values with Beef and Sour Cream

| Cal | Tot Fat | Sat Fat | Chol. | Potass | Carbs | Prot. | Fiber | Sugar |
|---|---|---|---|---|---|---|---|---|
| 592 | 29g | 9g | 82mg | 731mg | 43g | 38g | 3g | 3g |

→Nutritional values with Chicken and Sour Cream

| Cal | Tot Fat | Sat Fat | Chol. | Potass | Carbs | Prot. | Fiber | Sugar |
|---|---|---|---|---|---|---|---|---|
| 525 | 20g | 5g | 94mg | 564mg | 43g | 43g | 3g | 3g |

CARB X-change 3

**Total Sodium** per serving
Beef 435mg
Chicken 423mg

# Pecan-Crusted Salmon or Chicken

**Oven Temp:**
425°F

## Ingredients:

| | Chicken Sodium per serving | Salmon Sodium per serving |
|---|---|---|
| 4 - 4oz. Salmon Filets 🛒 or 4 - 6oz. Boneless, Skinless Chicken Breast 🛒 | 111mg | 64mg |
| 2oz. Chopped Pecans or No Sodium Almonds | | 0mg |
| ⅔ cup Plain Panko Bread Crumbs 🛒 | | 13mg |
| ¼ tsp. Paprika | | 0mg |
| ¼ cup Honey Dijon Mustard 🛒 | | 120mg |
| ¼ cup Honey | | 0mg |

### fyi:

**Frozen Chicken Breasts** will generally be higher in sodium than fresh.

Also, note that **fresh** and **frozen** chicken can be injected with sodium during the processing phase.

✓FAMILY FAVORITE

## How to:

Combine mustard and honey in a small bowl. Set aside.

Combine nuts, bread crumbs, and paprika in a small bowl. Set aside.

Spray shallow baking dish with non-stick spray.

Place salmon or chicken in dish and spoon honey-mustard mixture over meat.

Top with bread crumb-nut mixture.

Place in oven uncovered.

Cook salmon (15-20 min) or until done depending on thickness of fish. An internal temperature of 145°F is recommended.

Cook Chicken (30-40 min) or until done depending on thickness of meat. An internal temperature of 165°F is recommended.

If bread crumbs begin to burn a bit, finish cooking with dish covered in foil

Yields: 4 servings
(1 serving = 4 oz. salmon or 6 oz. chicken)

→Nutritional values with Chicken

| Cal | Tot Fat | Sat Fat | Chol. | Potass | Carbs | Prot. | Fiber | Sugar |
|---|---|---|---|---|---|---|---|---|
| 416 | 13g | 1g | 99mg | 506mg | 30g | 42g | 2g | 19g |

→Nutritional values with Salmon

| Cal | Tot Fat | Sat Fat | Chol. | Potass | Carbs | Prot. | Fiber | Sugar |
|---|---|---|---|---|---|---|---|---|
| 435 | 20g | 2g | 81mg | 784mg | 30g | 31g | 2g | 19g |

CARB X-change **2**

**Total Sodium** per serving
Beef 245mg
Chicken 198mg

# Baked Mahi-Mahi

## Ingredients:

| | Sodium per serving |
|---|---|
| 4 - 4 oz. Mahi-Mahi Filets | 127mg |
| 1 Lemon | 0mg |
| 3 Tbsp. Fresh Grated Parmesan Cheese 🛒 | 96mg |
| 2 Tbsp. Unsalted Butter | <1mg |
| 1½ Tbsp. Light Mayonnaise 🛒 | 23mg |
| 2 Tbsp. Green Onion, chopped | <1mg |
| ⅛ tsp. Black Pepper | 0mg |
| ⅓ cup Plain Panko Bread Crumbs 🛒 | 7mg |

## How to:

Place fish in large shallow baking dish and squeeze lemon juice over fish.

Place in oven and bake for 5 minutes.

Combine parmesan cheese, butter, mayonnaise, onion, and pepper in small bowl and brush over fish.

Sprinkle bread crumbs over fish evenly and cook for an additional 5-7 minutes or until fish flakes easily. An internal temperature of 145°F is recommended.

Yields: 4 servings (1 serving = 4 oz. fish)

**fyi:**

**Mayonnaise:** I have found the store brand is generally lower in sodium.

| Cal | Tot Fat | Sat Fat | Chol. | Potass | Carbs | Prot. | Fiber | Sugar |
|---|---|---|---|---|---|---|---|---|
| 211 | 10g | 5g | 122mg | 26mg | 2g | 29g | <1g | <1g |

CARB X-change 0

Total Sodium per serving 253mg

# Grilled Tuna Steak
## with Honey Mustard Marinade

## Ingredients:

| | Sodium per serving |
|---|---|
| ⅔ cup Red Wine Vinegar | 0mg |
| ⅓ cup Honey Dijon Mustard 🛒 | 120mg |
| 2 Tbsp. Honey | <1mg |
| 6 Tbsp. Extra Virgin Olive Oil | 0mg |
| 1 tsp. Garlic Herb Seasoning, (ex. Mrs. Dash) | 0mg |
| 4 - 4 oz. Tuna Steaks | 140mg |

## How to:

Combine all ingredients except tuna in a small bowl.

Place tuna steaks in medium storage bag and pour in mixture.

Marinate for at least 2 hours.

Grill Tuna on high heat 5-6 minutes each side depending on thickness of steaks.
An internal temperature of 145°F is recommended.

Yields: 4 servings (1 serving = 4 oz. of tuna)

☑ SUPER EASY

| Cal | Tot Fat | Sat Fat | Chol. | Potass | Carbs | Prot. | Fiber | Sugar |
|---|---|---|---|---|---|---|---|---|
| 462 | 35g | 8g | 68mg | 39mg | 10g | 26g | 0g | 9g |

CARB X-change ½

Total Sodium per serving
260mg

# Open Face
# Tuna Melts

Oven Temp:
Broil

## Ingredients:

| | Sodium per serving |
|---|---|
| 2 - 4.5 oz. Cans Very Low-Sodium Tuna, drained | 15mg |
| ¼ cup Light Mayonnaise | 60mg |
| ⅓ cup Celery, finely chopped | 9mg |
| 2 Tbsp. Green Onion, finely chopped | 0mg |
| ½ Tbsp. Fresh Parsley | 0mg |
| 1 tsp. Balsamic Vinegar | <1mg |
| ⅛ tsp. Black Pepper | 0mg |
| 4 Tomato Slices | <1mg |
| 2 English Muffins | 132mg |
| 4 Slices of Swiss Cheese | 49mg |
| Foil for easy clean up | |

## How to:

Combine tuna, mayonnaise, celery, onion, parsley, vinegar, and black pepper in a small bowl.

Toast both sides of the english muffins and place on sheet of foil next to each other.

Spoon tuna mixture on to the english muffins evenly and top each one with a slice of tomato and cheese.

Place on baking sheet and place in stove for a couple minutes until cheese melts. (Watch carefully)

Yields: 4 servings
(1 serving = 1 made up muffin)

┌─ **fyi:** ──────────────────────────
│ **Mayonnaise:** I have found the store
│ brand is generally lower in sodium.
└──────────────────────────────────

| Cal | Tot Fat | Sat Fat | Chol. | Potass | Carbs | Prot. | Fiber | Sugar |
|---|---|---|---|---|---|---|---|---|
| 240 | 10g | 4g | 38mg | 286mg | 15g | 21g | 1g | <1g |

CARB X-change 1

Total Sodium per serving
267mg

**69**
the **main** dish

# Tuna Patties

## Ingredients:

| | Sodium per serving |
|---|---|
| **1 - 4.5 oz Can of Very Low Sodium Tuna,** drained | 15mg |
| **2 Large Eggs,** beaten | 32mg |
| **1½ cups Plain Panko Bread Crumbs,** divided | 30mg |
| **3 Green Onions,** finely chopped | 4mg |
| **3 Tbsp. Celery,** finely chopped | 5mg |
| **2 tsp. Honey Dijon Mustard** | 20mg |
| **1 tsp. Lemon Juice** | 0mg |
| **¼ tsp. Black Pepper** | 0mg |
| **2 Tbsp. Olive Oil** | 0mg |

## How to:

Combine tuna, eggs, ⅔ cup Panko, onions, celery, mustard, lemon juice, and black pepper in a medium bowl.

Divide mixture into 4 equal balls and set aside to rest for a couple of minutes.

Place remaining Panko in shallow dish.

Heat olive oil in a large skillet on medium high.

Dip each ball into Panko and form into ½" patties.

Place in skillet and brown on each side cooking approximately 4- 5 minutes per side.

Yields: 4 servings   (1 serving = 1 tuna patty)

| Cal | Tot Fat | Sat Fat | Chol. | Potass | Carbs | Prot. | Fiber | Sugar |
|---|---|---|---|---|---|---|---|---|
| 307 | 10g | 2g | 166mg | 420mg | 21g | 32g | 1g | 2g |

CARB X-change 1½

Total Sodium per serving
106mg

# Tuna Salad

## Ingredients:

| | Sodium per serving |
|---|---|
| **2 - 4.5 oz. Cans Very Low-Sodium Tuna,** drained | 15mg |
| **¼ cup Celery,** finely chopped | 7mg |
| **3 Tbsp. Onion,** minced | <1mg |
| **2 Large Eggs,** hard boiled | 32mg |
| **½ cup Light Mayonnaise** | 120mg |
| **2 Tbsp. Low or No Sodium Sweet Pickle Relish** | 61mg |
| **¼ tsp. Garlic Powder** | 0mg |

## How to:

Combine all ingredients in a small bowl and mix well.

Yields: 4 servings  (1 serving = ½ cup)

## fyi:

**Mayonnaise:** I have found the store brand is generally lower in sodium.

| Cal | Tot Fat | Sat Fat | Chol. | Potass | Carbs | Prot. | Fiber | Sugar |
|---|---|---|---|---|---|---|---|---|
| 182 | 11g | 3g | 126mg | 229mg | 4g | 16g | <1g | <1g |

CARB X-change  0

Total Sodium per serving
235mg

# Garlic-Dill Salmon

**Oven Temp:**
375°F

## Ingredients:

| | Sodium per serving |
|---|---|
| Non-stick Spray | |
| 4 - 4 oz. Salmon Filets  | 63mg |
| ¼ cup Unsalted Butter, melted | 2mg |
| 1 Tbsp. Garlic, finely minced | <1mg |
| 2 Tbsp. Fresh Dill, minced | <1mg |
| 1 tsp. Fresh Rosemary (optional) | 0mg |
| 1 Lemon, cut into ¼ in. slices | 0mg |
| Pepper to taste | 0mg |

## How to:

Spray baking dish large enough to hold salmon with non-stick spray.

In a small bowl, mix unsalted butter, garlic, dill, and rosemary.

Place salmon in dish and place butter mixture evenly over salmon filets.

Sprinkle with pepper to taste then top each one with a lemon slice.

Bake in oven for 15-20 minutes or until fish flakes easily. An internal temperature of 145°F is recommended.

**Suggestion:** Serve with rice and use extra lemon slices to squeeze over fish once baked.

Yields: 4 (1 serving = 4 oz. salmon)

✓ SUPER EASY

→Nutritional is figured without rice.

| Cal | Tot Fat | Sat Fat | Chol. | Potass | Carbs | Prot. | Fiber | Sugar |
|---|---|---|---|---|---|---|---|---|
| 317 | 21g | 9g | 112mg | 766mg | 4g | 29g | 1g | 0g |

CARB X-change 0

Total Sodium per serving
66mg

# Broiled Salmon

## Ingredients:

|  | Sodium per serving |
|---|---|
| Non-stick spray | |
| 4 - 4 oz. Salmon Filets  | 63mg |
| 4 Tbsp. Jalapeño Jelly | 0mg |

## How to:

Spray broiling rack with non-stick spray and align salmon filets on rack.

Place salmon in oven and broil for 8-9 minutes or until fish reaches an internal temperature of 145°F.

When fish is done, add a Tbsp. of jelly to each piece of salmon.

Broil and continue to cook for another 30 seconds or until jelly just starts to melt.

Yields:  4 servings (1 serving = 4 oz. salmon)

**cooking tip**
Make sure top rack of oven is 5-6 " from broiler and open up the oven door every 1-2 minutes to ensure that fish does not burn.

✓ SUPER EASY

✓ FAMILY FAVORITE

| Cal | Tot Fat | Sat Fat | Chol. | Potass | Carbs | Prot. | Fiber | Sugar |
|---|---|---|---|---|---|---|---|---|
| 256 | 9g | 1g | 81mg | 712mg | 11g | 29g | 0g | 8g |

CARB X-change 0

Total Sodium per serving
63mg

# Shrimp Scampi

## Ingredients:

| | Sodium per serving |
|---|---|
| **20-25 Large Fresh Shrimp,** cooked | 154mg |
| **1½ cups Fresh Spinach** | 18mg |
| **2 tsp. Extra Virgin Olive Oil** | 0mg |
| **2 Cloves Garlic,** minced | 0mg |
| **1 tsp. Fresh Basil** | 0mg |
| **¼ tsp. Black Pepper** | 0mg |

## How to:

Combine all ingredients in large skillet over medium heat. Mix well.

**Suggestion:** Serve with rice.

Yields:  2 servings (1 serving = 10-12 shrimp)

☑ SUPER EASY

→Nutritional is figured without rice

| Cal | Tot Fat | Sat Fat | Chol. | Potass | Carbs | Prot. | Fiber | Sugar |
|---|---|---|---|---|---|---|---|---|
| 118 | 6g | <1g | 134mg | 268mg | 2g | 15g | <1g | <1g |

CARB X-change 0

Total Sodium per serving
172mg

# Shrimp Creole

## Ingredients:

| | Sodium per serving |
|---|---|
| ¼ cup **Onion**, chopped | <1mg |
| 2 **Garlic Cloves**, minced | <1mg |
| 1 **Tbsp. Extra Virgin Olive Oil** | <1mg |
| ¼ cup **Celery**, diced | <1mg |
| 2 tsp. **Fresh Parsley**, minced | <1mg |
| 1 tsp. **Sugar** | 0mg |
| 1 **Whole Bay Leaf** | 0mg |
| ½ cup **Green Pepper**, chopped | <1mg |
| 1 - 6 oz. **Can of NSA Tomato Paste** | 26mg |
| 1½ cups **Water** | 0mg |
| 12 oz. **Fresh Shrimp**, medium | 190mg |
| **Cayenne Pepper to taste**, (optional) | 0mg |

## How to:

Add oil, onions, and garlic in a medium pot and saute' until soft.

Mix in remaining ingredients except shrimp.

Heat on low for 20 minutes.

Add shrimp and cook for 10-15 minutes until shrimp are done.

**Suggestion:** Serve with rice.

Yields: 4 servings
(1 serving = about 10 Shrimp
with about a ¾ cup of liquid.)

---

**fyi:**

**Chicken Broth:** For an even lower sodium recipe use recipe on page 27.

---

→Nutritional is figured without rice

| Cal | Tot Fat | Sat Fat | Chol. | Potass | Carbs | Prot. | Fiber | Sugar |
|---|---|---|---|---|---|---|---|---|
| 159 | 4g | <1g | 166mg | 530mg | 10g | 19g | 5g | 5g |

CARB X-change ½

Total Sodium per serving
218mg

# Oven Fried Catfish

## Ingredients:

| | Sodium per serving |
|---|---|
| 2 Tbsp. Flour | 0mg |
| 2 tsp. Paprika, divided | 0mg |
| 1½ tsp. Garlic Powder, divided | 0mg |
| ¼ tsp. Black Pepper | 0mg |
| ⅛ tsp. Cayenne Pepper | 0mg |
| ⅔ cup Yellow Corn Meal | 0mg |
| 2 Egg Whites | 28mg |
| 4 - 4 oz. Catfish Fillets | 91mg |
| Non-Stick Cooking Spray | |

## How to:

In a shallow dish combine flour, 1 tsp. paprika, and ½ tsp. garlic powder. Set aside.

In another shallow dish combine 1 tsp. paprika, 1 tsp. garlic powder, black pepper, cayenne pepper, and corn meal.

Place egg whites in a shallow dish.

Spray baking sheet with cooking spray.

Dip (1 piece at a time) catfish in flour mixture; then in egg whites; and finally in cornmeal mixture. Place on baking sheet.

After all catfish fillets are on baking sheet, spray catfish lightly with cooking spray.

Cook 6-7 minutes. Flip and spray catfish again and cook for 6-7 more minutes or until fish flakes.

Yields:  4 servings  (1 serving = 4 oz. catfish)

| Cal | Tot Fat | Sat Fat | Chol. | Potass | Carbs | Prot. | Fiber | Sugar |
|---|---|---|---|---|---|---|---|---|
| 285 | 10g | 2g | 73mg | 434mg | 24g | 26g | 3g | <1g |

CARB X-change 1½

Total Sodium
119mg per serving

# Steak Topped with Crab

## Ingredients:

| | Sodium per serving |
|---|---|
| **4 - 6 oz. Steaks,** (thick sirloin works well) | 112mg |
| **⅓ cup Half-n-Half or Whipping Cream** | 8mg |
| **1.5 oz. Low-Fat Cream Cheese** | 31mg |
| **2 Tbsp. Green Onions,** thinly sliced | <1mg |
| **½ tsp. Herb Pepper Seasoning** (ex. Mrs. Dash) | 0mg |
| **2 oz. Fresh Flaked Crab Meat** | 120mg |
| **1½ tsp. Fresh Lemon Juice** | 0mg |
| **¼ tsp. Seafood Seasoning** | 95mg |
| **⅛ tsp. Black Pepper** | 0mg |

## How to:

Place steaks on grill and cook to desired temperature. An internal temperature of 145° is recommended.

While steaks cook, combine remaining ingredients in small saucepan on low heat until thickened.

Top steaks with sauce and serve.

Yields: 4 servings (1 serving = 6 oz. steak)

| Cal | Tot Fat | Sat Fat | Chol. | Potass | Carbs | Prot. | Fiber | Sugar |
|---|---|---|---|---|---|---|---|---|
| 396 | 18g | 8g | 165mg | 766mg | 2g | 53g | <1g | <1g |

CARB X-change 0

Total Sodium per serving
376mg

# Sloppy Joes

## Ingredients:

| | Beef Sodium per serving | Turkey Sodium per serving |
|---|---|---|
| 1 lb. Lean Ground Beef or Ground Turkey | 37mg | 43mg |
| ¼ cup Onion, chopped | | <1mg |
| ¼ cup Green Pepper, chopped | | <1mg |
| 1 cup NSA Ketchup | | 10mg |
| 4 tsp. Brown Sugar | | 1mg |
| 1¼ tsp. Worcestershire Sauce 🛒 | | 7mg |
| ¾ tsp. Mustard Powder | | 0mg |
| ¾ tsp. Garlic Powder | | 0mg |
| ¾ tsp. Chili Powder 🛒 | | 4mg |
| ½ tsp. Black Pepper | | 0mg |
| ½ tsp. Celery Seed | | 2mg |
| 8 Hamburger Buns 🛒 | | 206mg |

## How to:

Brown ground beef or turkey in a large skillet.

Drain and add onion and green pepper.

In a small bowl, add ketchup, brown sugar, worcestershire, mustard powder, garlic powder, chili powder, black pepper, and celery seed.

Stir to combine.

Add to meat mixture and heat on low for 15-20 minutes.

Yields: 8 servings

(1 serving = ½ cup serving with bun)

## fyi:

**Chili Powder:** A no sodium chili powder is available in specialty stores or see recipe on page 5.

**Brown Sugar:** For a healthier recipe, an equivalent brown sugar substitute may be substituted for brown sugar.

→Nutritional values with Beef

| Cal | Tot Fat | Sat Fat | Chol. | Potass | Carbs | Prot. | Fiber | Sugar |
|---|---|---|---|---|---|---|---|---|
| 333 | 14g | 5g | 43mg | 553mg | 37g | 14g | 1g | 11g |

→Nutritional values with Turkey

| Cal | Tot Fat | Sat Fat | Chol. | Potass | Carbs | Prot. | Fiber | Sugar |
|---|---|---|---|---|---|---|---|---|
| 263 | 6g | 2g | 40mg | 405mg | 37g | 15g | 1g | 11g |

CARB X-change 2½

Total Sodium per serving
Beef 269mg
Turkey 263mg

# Meatloaf

## Ingredients:

| Ingredients | Beef Sodium per serving | Turkey Sodium per serving |
|---|---|---|
| 1lb. Extra Lean Ground Beef or 1lb. Ground Turkey | 39mg | 40mg |
| ¾ cup Oats | | <1mg |
| ½ cup Onion, chopped | | <1mg |
| ¼ cup Celery, chopped | | 3mg |
| ½ cup NSA Ketchup | | 8mg |
| 1 large Egg | | 8mg |
| 1 Tbsp. Worcestershire Sauce | | 21mg |
| 2 Garlic Cloves, minced | | <1mg |
| ¼ tsp. Black Pepper | | 0mg |
| ¼ tsp. Dried Basil | | 0mg |

### Topping: (optional)

| | Beef Sodium | Turkey Sodium |
|---|---|---|
| 1½ Tbsp. Brown Sugar, packed | | <1mg |
| ¼ cup NSA Ketchup | | 3mg |
| 1 tsp. Mustard Powder | | 0mg |
| ⅛ tsp. Nutmeg | | 0mg |
| ¼ tsp. Onion Powder | | 0mg |

## How to:

Combine all ingredients in a large bowl.

Mix gently but thoroughly.

Place mixture into 10" x 6" loaf pan.

Bake uncovered 50 minutes to 1 hour or until internal temperature reaches of 160°F.

Add topping 20 minutes before taking out of oven.

Slice into 8 equal slices.

Yields:  8 servings  (1 serving = 1 slice)

## fyi:

**Brown Sugar:** For a healthier recipe, an equivalent brown sugar substitute may be substituted for brown sugar.

→Nutritional values with Beef and Topping

| Cal | Tot Fat | Sat Fat | Chol. | Potass | Carbs | Prot. | Fiber | Sugar |
|---|---|---|---|---|---|---|---|---|
| 238 | 13g | 5g | 69mg | 512mg | 23g | 12g | 2g | 2g |

→Nutritional values with Turkey and Topping

| Cal | Tot Fat | Sat Fat | Chol. | Potass | Carbs | Prot. | Fiber | Sugar |
|---|---|---|---|---|---|---|---|---|
| 168 | 5g | 2g | 67mg | 364mg | 23g | 13g | 2g | 2g |

CARB X-change 1 ½

Total Sodium per serving
Beef    80mg
Turkey  83mg

# Spaghetti Bake

**Oven Temp:** 350°F

## Ingredients:

| Ingredient | Beef Sodium per serving | Turkey Sodium per serving |
|---|---|---|
| 2 Tbsp. Extra Virgin Olive Oil | | 0mg |
| 1 cup Onion, finely chopped | | <1mg |
| 4 Garlic Cloves, minced | | <1mg |
| 2 - 14.5oz. cans NSA Diced Tomatoes or 4 cups Tomatoes, peeled and seeded | | 44mg |
| 1 - 6oz. can of NSA Tomato Paste | | 6mg |
| 2½ tsp. Sugar | | 0mg |
| 1 tsp. Dried Basil or 1 Tbsp. Fresh Basil | | 0mg |
| ½ tsp. Dried Oregano or ½ Tbsp. Fresh Oregano | | 0mg |
| ½ tsp. Black Pepper | | 0mg |
| 1 Bay Leaf | | 0mg |
| 12oz. Spaghetti Noodles | | 0mg |
| 1lb. Lean Ground Beef or 1lb. Ground Turkey | 39mg | 43mg |
| 1 cup Fresh Mushrooms, sliced | | <1mg |
| 8oz. Fresh Mozzarella, diced and divided | | 85mg |
| ¼ cup Reduced Fat Parmesan Cheese | | 64mg |

## How to:

In a medium saucepan add olive oil, onion, and garlic and cook until soft.

Add tomatoes, tomato paste, sugar, basil, oregano, and black pepper to pan and simmer on low for 20-30 minutes, stirring occasionally.

Cook pasta for 8 minutes in boiling water. Set aside.

Brown ground beef or turkey. Set aside.

In a large bowl combine noodles, sauce, ground beef or turkey, mushrooms, and 4 oz. mozzarella .

Pour into a 9 "x 13" baking dish and top with remaining mozzarella and parmesan cheese.

Cover with foil and bake 45 minutes.

Cut into 8 equal portions.

Yields: 8 servings  (1 serving = 1 portion)

→Nutritional values with Beef

| Cal | Tot Fat | Sat Fat | Chol. | Potass | Carbs | Prot. | Fiber | Sugar |
|---|---|---|---|---|---|---|---|---|
| 473 | 23g | 9g | 66mg | 217mg | 43g | 24g | 5g | 8g |

→Nutritional values with Turkey

| Cal | Tot Fat | Sat Fat | Chol. | Potass | Carbs | Prot. | Fiber | Sugar |
|---|---|---|---|---|---|---|---|---|
| 403 | 14g | 6g | 64mg | 69mg | 43g | 25g | 5g | 8g |

CARB X-change **3**

**Total Sodium** per serving
Beef 239mg
Turkey 242mg

# Lasagna

## Ingredients:

| | Beef Sodium per serving | Turkey Sodium per serving |
|---|---|---|
| **9 Lasagna Noodles,** uncooked | | 38mg |
| **1lb. Ground Lean Beef or 1lb. Ground Turkey** | 35mg | 38mg |
| **1 Tbsp. Olive Oil** | | 0mg |
| **¾ cup Onion,** chopped | | <1mg |
| **5 Garlic Cloves,** minced | | 0mg |
| **1 - 14.5 oz. can NSA Diced Tomatoes** | | 19mg |
| **1 - 6 oz. can NSA Tomato Paste** | | 6mg |
| **1 tsp. Basil** | | 0mg |
| **1½ tsp. Oregano** | | 0mg |
| **1 tsp. Thyme** | | 0mg |
| **½ tsp. Black Pepper** | | 0mg |
| **1 Large Egg,** beaten | | 7mg |
| **1 - 15 oz. container Fat Free Ricotta Cheese** | | 50mg |
| **¼ cup Parmesan Cheese** | | 57mg |
| **8 oz. Fresh Mozzarella,** (preferrably packed in water), shred or cut into small pieces | | 44mg |

**fyi:**

Fresh **Mozzarella** contains less sodium than shredded and packaged Mozzarella.

## How to:

Cook noodles according to package directions (minus the salt) and cut noodles in half after cooked.

In a large skillet brown meat and drain fat.

In a medium sauce pan, cook onion and garlic in olive oil until tender. Then, add tomato sauce, basil, Italian seasoning, and black pepper. Let simmer for 20-25 minutes.

Add browned ground beef to sauce.

In a medium bowl combine ricotta cheese, egg, and parmesan.

Spray 8" x 8" dish with non-stick spray.

Spread a thin layer of meat sauce on bottom of dish.

Repeat the following layering 3 times except leave off the top layer of mozzarella to be added last 15 minutes of cooking.
1. 3 noodles side by side
2. ⅓ of meat sauce on top of noodles
3. ⅓ of Cheese mixture
4. then ⅓ of the mozzarella.

Bake for 50 minutes.
Let cool 10-15 minutes before serving.
Cut into 9 equal portions.
Yields: 9 servings (1 serving = 1 portion)

→Nutritional values with Beef

| Cal | Tot Fat | Sat Fat | Chol. | Potass | Carbs | Prot. | Fiber | Sugar |
|---|---|---|---|---|---|---|---|---|
| 358 | 19g | 8g | 88mg | 175mg | 22g | 23g | 3g | 5g |

→Nutritional values with Turkey

| Cal | Tot Fat | Sat Fat | Chol. | Potass | Carbs | Prot. | Fiber | Sugar |
|---|---|---|---|---|---|---|---|---|
| 296 | 12g | 5g | 85mg | 43mg | 22g | 24g | 3g | 5g |

CARB X-change 1½

**Total Sodium per serving**
Beef 219mg
Turkey 222mg

# Slow Cooker Chili

**Slow Cooker:**

| Ingredients: | Beef Sodium per serving | Turkey Sodium per serving |
|---|---|---|
| 2 lb. Extra Lean Ground Beef or Ground Turkey | 78mg | 85mg |
| 2 - 8 oz. cans NSA Tomato Sauce | | 13mg |
| 2 - 14.5 oz. cans Kidney Beans | | 75mg |
| 2 - 14.5 oz. cans Pinto Beans | | 75mg |
| 1 cup Onion, chopped | | <1mg |
| 1 - 4 oz. can Green Chiles | | 38mg |
| ½ cup Celery, chopped | | 3mg |
| 3 Garlic Cloves, minced | | <1mg |
| 2 - 14.5 oz. cans NSA Diced Tomatoes | | 38mg |
| 2½ tsp. Cumin | | 0mg |
| 2-3 Tbsp. Chili Powder (or to taste) | | 45mg |
| 1 tsp. Black Pepper | | 0mg |
| 1 tsp. Oregano | | 0mg |
| 1 tsp. Paprika | | 0mg |
| 1 tsp. Sugar | | 0mg |

## How to:

Brown ground beef or turkey in skillet.

Add all ingredients in slow cooker.

Stir.

Let cook for 8-9 hours on low.

Yields: 8 servings (1 serving = 1 cup)

## fyi:

**Beans:** Shop around to find lowest sodium beans. Draining and rinsing the beans will help lower the sodium content.

**Chili Powder:** A no sodium chili powder is available in specialty stores or see recipe on page 5.

**Sugar:** For a healthier recipe, an equivalent sugar substitute may be substituted for sugar.

→Nutritional values with Beef

| Cal | Tot Fat | Sat Fat | Chol. | Potass | Carbs | Prot. | Fiber | Sugar |
|---|---|---|---|---|---|---|---|---|
| 501 | 24g | 10g | 85mg | 398mg | 42g | 32g | 11g | 8g |

→Nutritional values with Turkey

| Cal | Tot Fat | Sat Fat | Chol. | Potass | Carbs | Prot. | Fiber | Sugar |
|---|---|---|---|---|---|---|---|---|
| 360 | 8g | 3g | 80mg | 102mg | 42g | 34g | 11g | 8g |

CARB X-change **3**

**Total Sodium** per serving
Beef 367mg
Chicken 377mg

# Stromboli

## Ingredients:

| | Beef Sodium per serving | Turkey Sodium per serving |
|---|---|---|
| **1 lb. Lean Ground Beef or Ground Turkey** | 75mg | 88mg |
| **¼ cup Onion,** chopped | | <1mg |
| **½ cup NSA Ketchup** | | 0mg |
| **2 Tbsp. Parmesan Cheese,** freshly grated  | | 47mg |
| **3½ tsp. Garlic Powder** | | 0mg |
| **½ tsp Thyme** | | 0mg |
| **½ tsp. Oregano** | | 0mg |
| **½ tsp. Red Pepper Flakes,** (optional) | | 0mg |
| **4 Tbsp. Unsalted Butter** | | 2mg |
| **4 Kaiser or Hoagie Buns** | | 300mg |
| **8 oz. Fresh Mozzarella** | | 50mg |

## How to:

Brown ground beef or turkey in skillet. Drain

In a small bowl mix onion, ketchup, parmesan cheese, 1½ tsp. garlic powder, thyme and oregano, and red pepper flakes.

Pour over and mix with meat in skillet.

Melt 4 Tbsp. unsalted butter in a small bowl and add 2 tsp. garlic powder.

Brush butter on all sides of rolls.

Spread 1 oz. mozzarella on bottom roll.

Place ¼ of meat mixture on roll.

Top with 1 oz. of mozzarella.

When assembled, wrap in foil sprayed with non-stick oil and bake in oven for 20 minutes.

Yields:  4 servings
(1 serving = 1 made-up sandwich)

## fyi:

**Fresh Mozzarella** contains less sodium than shredded and packaged Mozzarella.

→Nutritional values with Beef

| Cal | Tot Fat | Sat Fat | Chol. | Potass | Carbs | Prot. | Fiber | Sugar |
|---|---|---|---|---|---|---|---|---|
| 732 | 43g | 23g | 141mg | 716mg | 47g | 33g | 5g | 13g |

→Nutritional values with Turkey

| Cal | Tot Fat | Sat Fat | Chol. | Potass | Carbs | Prot. | Fiber | Sugar |
|---|---|---|---|---|---|---|---|---|
| 660 | 26g | 20g | 147mg | 616mg | 47g | 44g | 5g | 13g |

CARB X-change 3

**Total Sodium per serving**
Beef 472mg
Turkey 484mg

# Pork Kabobs

## Ingredients:

| | Sodium per serving |
|---|---|
| 1 lb. **Pork Tenderloin,** cut into 1" squares | 62mg |
| 2 Tbsp. **Low Sodium** 🛒 **Teriyaki Sauce** | 160mg |
| 2 Tbsp. **Red Wine Vinegar** | 3mg |
| 2 Tbsp. **Canola Oil** | 0mg |
| 2 tsp. **Brown Sugar** | 1mg |
| ½ tsp. **Red Pepper Flakes,** (optional) | 0mg |
| 1 **Red Bell Pepper,** cut into 1" squares | 1mg |
| ½ **Red Onion,** cut into 1" squares | 1mg |
| 1 - 8 oz. can of **Pineapple Chunks** | 5mg |

## fyi:

**Brown Sugar:** For a healthier recipe, an equivalent brown sugar substitute may be substituted for brown sugar.

## How to:

Combine teriyaki sauce, vinegar, oil, brown sugar, and red pepper flakes in a small bowl.

Place cut up pork and vegetables in a resealable bag.

Add liquid mixture and place in refrigerator for 5-6 hours.

When ready to cook, get 4 skewers and thread meat and vegetables on skewers, alternating onion, pork, pineapple, bell pepper and so on.

Place on grill or broil in oven until meat reaches an internal temperature of 165°F.

**Suggestion:** Serve with rice.

Yields: 4 servings (1 serving = 1 kabob)

→Nutritional is figured without rice

| Cal | Tot Fat | Sat Fat | Chol. | Potass | Carbs | Prot. | Fiber | Sugar |
|---|---|---|---|---|---|---|---|---|
| 356 | 16g | 3g | 90mg | 656mg | 17g | 34g | 4g | 13g |

CARB X-change 1

Total Sodium 233mg per serving

# Honey Pecan Pork Chops

## Ingredients:

| | Sodium per serving |
|---|---|
| ½ cup Flour | <1mg |
| ¼ tsp. Black Pepper | 0mg |
| ¼ tsp. Onion Powder | 0mg |
| ¼ tsp. Garlic Powder | 0mg |
| ¼ tsp. Paprika | 0mg |
| 4 Boneless Pork Chops, ½" thick | 46mg |
| 2 Tbsp. Unsalted Butter | <1mg |
| ¼ cup Pecans, chopped | 0mg |
| ¼ cup Honey | <1mg |
| 3 Tbsp. Onion, finely chopped | <1mg |
| 1 Tbsp. Honey Dijon Mustard | 30mg |

## How to:

In a shallow dish, add flour, pepper, onion powder, garlic powder, and paprika.

Heat unsalted butter in a large skillet on medium-high heat.

Dip pork chops in flour mixture and shake off excess.

Place in skillet and brown on each side for 10-12 minutes.

In a medium bowl, add remaining ingredients.

Once pork chops are done remove from skillet, reduce heat, and add honey mixture.

Heat for 2-3 minutes, and add pork chops back to skillet.

Spoon sauce over pork chops.

Yields: 4 servings (1 serving = 1 pork chop)

| Cal | Tot Fat | Sat Fat | Chol. | Potass | Carbs | Prot. | Fiber | Sugar |
|---|---|---|---|---|---|---|---|---|
| 424 | 22g | 8g | 75mg | 482mg | 32g | 23g | 1g | 18g |

CARB X-change 2

Total Sodium per serving
76mg

# Smothered Pork Chops

## Ingredients:

| | Sodium per serving |
|---|---|
| 4 - ½-¾" Pork Chops | 44mg |
| ½ cup All Purpose Flour | <1mg |
| 1 Tbsp. Garlic Powder | <1mg |
| 1 Tbsp. Onion Powder | <1mg |
| 1 Tbsp. Dried Parsley | <1mg |
| ½ Tbsp. Black Pepper | 0mg |
| ¼ cup Olive Oil | 0mg |
| 1 cup Low Sodium Chicken Broth  | 113mg |
| ½ cup Skim Milk | 16mg |
| 1 Tbsp. Browning and Seasoning Sauce | 3mg |
| 1½ cups Fresh Mushrooms, thinly sliced | 1mg |

## fyi:

**Chicken Broth:** For an even lower sodium recipe, use recipe on page 27.

## How to:

In a shallow dish mix flour, garlic powder, onion powder, parsley, and pepper.

Dip pork chops in flour mixture and shake off excess.

Heat olive oil over medium-high heat in a large skillet and add pork chops.

Cover and cook 4-5 minutes on each side or until pork chops are golden brown.

Remove pork chops from skillet, add 3-4 Tbsp. of flour mixture to pan, and whisk for a couple of minutes.

Add chicken broth and continue to whisk until thickened.

Finally add milk, browning sauce, and mushrooms and continue to stir until well combined.

Add pork chops back to pan, cover, and cook an additional 10-15 minutes until pork chops are done. An internal temperature of 160°F is recommended.

Yields: 4 servings (1 serving= 1 pork chop)

| Cal | Tot Fat | Sat Fat | Chol. | Potass | Carbs | Prot. | Fiber | Sugar |
|---|---|---|---|---|---|---|---|---|
| 408 | 25g | 6g | 60mg | 606mg | 20g | 25g | 1g | 30g |

CARB X-change 1

Total Sodium per serving
184mg

# Slow Cooker
# BBQ Pork

## Ingredients:

|  | Sodium per serving |
| --- | --- |
| 5-6 lb. Pork Butt | 137mg |
| 1 Tbsp. Extra Virgin Olive Oil | 0mg |
| ½ cup Onion, minced | 0mg |
| 5 Garlic Cloves | 25mg |
| ½ cup Brown Sugar, packed | <1mg |
| 2 Tbsp. Worcestershire Sauce | 17mg |
| 2 cups NSA Ketchup | <1mg |
| ½ cup Cider Vinegar | 4mg |
| 1 tsp. Garlic Powder | 0mg |
| 1 tsp. Onion Powder | 0mg |
| 1 Tbsp. Liquid Smoke | 17mg |
| 1½ tsp. Paprika | <1mg |
| 1¼ tsp. Dry Mustard | <1mg |
| ½ tsp. Black Pepper | 4mg |
| Non-Stick Cooking Spray | |

## How to:

Spray inside of slow cooker with non-stick spray.

Place pork butt in slow cooker.

Mix remaining ingredients in a medium size bowl and pour over pork butt.

Cook for 8-10 hours on low.

Yields: 8 servings (1 serving = Approx. 10 oz.)

## fyi:

**Brown Sugar:** For a healthier recipe, an equivalent brown sugar substitute may be substituted for brown sugar.

☑ FAMILY FAVORITE

| Cal | Tot Fat | Sat Fat | Chol. | Potass | Carbs | Prot. | Fiber | Sugar |
| --- | --- | --- | --- | --- | --- | --- | --- | --- |
| 977 | 70g | 25g | 266mg | 1024mg | 22g | 67g | <1g | 20g |

CARB X-change 1½

**Total Sodium** 205mg per serving

# Maple Glazed Pork Tenderloin

**Oven Temp:**
350°F

## Ingredients:

| Ingredient | Sodium per serving |
|---|---|
| 1½ lbs. Pork Tenderloin | 94mg |
| 1 cup Pure Maple Syrup | 5mg |
| 3 Tbsp. Honey Dijon Mustard | 135mg |
| 2 Tbsp. Olive Oil | 0mg |
| ½ tsp. Black Pepper | 0mg |
| ½ tsp. Dried Rosemary | 0mg |

☑ SUPER EASY

## How to:

Place all ingredients in a resealable bag and marinate overnight.

Place tenderloin in a 9" x 13" baking dish and cover with foil.

Bake 30-40 minutes or until meat reaches an internal temperature of 160°F.

Pour remaining marinade into a small sauce pan. Heat on low until sauce reaches a boil.

When meat is done, let rest for 10 minutes

Slice and serve with sauce.

Yields: 4 servings  (1 serving = 6 oz.)

| Cal | Tot Fat | Sat Fat | Chol. | Potass | Carbs | Prot. | Fiber | Sugar |
|---|---|---|---|---|---|---|---|---|
| 633 | 21g | 5g | 134mg | 741mg | 56g | 50g | 4g | 53g |

CARB X-change 4

Total Sodium per serving
234mg

# Grilled Pork Tenderloin Sandwiches

## Ingredients:

| | Sodium per serving |
|---|---|
| 1½ lb. Pork Tenderloin | 94mg |
| ¼ cup Olive Oil | 0mg |
| 3 Garlic Cloves | <1mg |
| 1 tsp. Dried Rosemary | 0mg |
| ½ tsp. Black Pepper | 0mg |
| 4 Hamburger Buns | 210mg |

## How to:

Flatten pork with a meat tenderizer until ½" thick. (Most grocery stores will do this at no cost if you want to skip this step)

Cut into 5" x 5" inch squares and place in resealable bag along with olive oil, garlic, rosemary, and black pepper. Let marinate 2-4 hours.

Grill for 15-20 minutes on medium heat until done.

Yields:  4 servings (1 serving = 1 sandwich)

☑ SUPER EASY

| Cal | Tot Fat | Sat Fat | Chol. | Potass | Carbs | Prot. | Fiber | Sugar |
|---|---|---|---|---|---|---|---|---|
| 586 | 29g | 6g | 134mg | 791mg | 22g | 54g | 5g | 3g |

CARB X-change 0

Total Sodium per serving
304mg

# Green Chile Burgers

## Ingredients:

| | Sodium per serving |
|---|---|
| **1 lb. Lean Ground Beef** | 78mg |
| **4 Slices of Swiss Cheese** | 74mg |
| **¼ cup Red Onion,** minced | <1mg |
| **1 Anaheim Pepper,** minced | 0mg |
| **1 Pablano Pepper,** minced | 0mg |
| **¼ tsp. Garlic Powder** | 0mg |
| **½ tsp. Black Pepper** | 0mg |
| | |
| **4 Hamburger Buns** | 206mg |

## How to:

Grill peppers for 10-15 minutes or until they start to brown.

Place peppers in resealable bag and let rest for 15 minutes.

While waiting for peppers, divide beef into 4 -4 oz. balls and form into patties.

Cook on grill until desired doneness.

While burgers are cooking, remove peppers from bag and peel off skin. (Remove seeds if desired) Mince peppers and mix in garlic powder.

When burgers are done, before taking off grill, top each with a Tbsp. of red onion and 1 slice of cheese.

When cheese is melted, place on bun and top cheese with ¼ of pepper mixture.

Yields:  4 servings  (1 serving = 1 burger with bun)

✓ SUPER EASY

| Cal | Tot Fat | Sat Fat | Chol. | Potass | Carbs | Prot. | Fiber | Sugar |
|---|---|---|---|---|---|---|---|---|
| 551 | 34g | 15g | 111mg | 391mg | 28g | 33g | 2g | 3g |

CARB X-change 2

Total Sodium per serving
358mg

# Turkey Burgers

## Ingredients:

|  | Sodium per serving |
|---|---|
| 1 lb. Lean Ground Turkey | 85mg |
| ½ cup Plain Panko Bread Crumbs 🛒 | 10mg |
| ½ cup Mushrooms, finely chopped | <1mg |
| ⅓ cup Green Onion, finely chopped | 1mg |
| ⅓ cup Red Bell Pepper, finely chopped | <1mg |
| 1½ tsp. Worcestershire Sauce 🛒 | 17mg |
| 1 tsp. Liquid Smoke | 3mg |
| 1 Large Egg | 16mg |
| 4 Hamburger Buns 🛒 | 206mg |

## How to:

Combine all ingredients into a small bowl and divide into 4 equal parts.

Form into patties and grill until done.

Yields: 4 servings (1 serving = 1 sandwich)

☑ SUPER EASY

| Cal | Tot Fat | Sat Fat | Chol. | Potass | Carbs | Prot. | Fiber | Sugar |
|---|---|---|---|---|---|---|---|---|
| 335 | 11g | 3g | 133mg | 106mg | 29g | 29g | 2g | 4g |

CARB X-change 2

Total Sodium 338mg per serving

# Black Bean Burgers

## Ingredients:

| | Sodium per serving |
|---|---|
| 2 - 16 oz. cans Black Beans | 136mg |
| ¼ cup Onion, minced | <1mg |
| ¼ cup Red Bell Pepper, minced | <1mg |
| 3 Garlic Cloves, minced | <1mg |
| 2 Large Eggs | 25mg |
| 1 tsp. Cumin | 0mg |
| 1 tsp. Chili Powder | 5mg |
| 2 tsp. Tobasco Sauce | 14mg |
| 1 cup Plain Panko Bread Crumbs | 18mg |
| 5 Hamburger Buns | 205mg |

### fyi:

**Beans:** Shop around to find lowest sodium beans. Draining and rinsing the beans will help lower the sodium content.

**Chili Powder:** A no sodium chili powder is available in specialty stores, or see recipe on page 5.

☑ SUPER EASY

## How to:

Drain and rinse beans. Mash with fork in a large bowl.

Add remaining ingredients except buns and form into five equal patties.

Grill for about 8-10 minutes per side or bake on 375°F for 15-20 minutes.

Serve with sliced avocado, tomato, lettuce and chipotle mayonnaise (Optional)
(See recipe in book on page 23.)

Yields: 5 servings (1 serving = 1 burger with bun)

| Cal | Tot Fat | Sat Fat | Chol. | Potass | Carbs | Prot. | Fiber | Sugar |
|---|---|---|---|---|---|---|---|---|
| 398 | 4g | 1g | 85mg | 102mg | 69g | 21g | 9g | 6g |

**CARB X-change** 4 ½

**Total Sodium per serving** 406mg

# Portabella Mushroom Burgers

## Ingredients:

| | Sodium per serving |
|---|---|
| **4 - Large Portabella Mushroom Caps** (about 5" in diameter) | 10mg |
| **2 Tbsp. Balsamic Vinegar** | 3mg |
| **3 Tbsp. Olive Oil** | 0mg |
| **½ tsp. Oregano** | 0mg |
| **¼ tsp. Coriander** | 0mg |
| **3 Garlic Cloves**, minced | <1mg |
| **¼ tsp. Black Pepper** | 0mg |
| **2 Tbsp. Fresh Basil** | 0mg |
| **½ cup Tomatoes**, chopped | 2mg |
| **4 slices Provolone Cheese** | 170mg |
| **4 Hamburger Buns** | 205mg |

## How to:

Wash mushrooms and dry.

Combine vinegar, olive oil, oregano, coriander, garlic, and pepper in a small bowl.

Place mushrooms in a large resealable bag and add vinegar mixture. Marinate 1 hour.

Place on grill cap side up for 7-8 minutes

Turn over and grill another 7-8 minutes then add 2 Tbsp. tomatoes, ½ Tbsp. basil, and a slice of cheese on top of each mushroom.

Yields:  4 servings (1 serving = 1 burger on bun)

| Cal | Tot Fat | Sat Fat | Chol. | Potass | Carbs | Prot. | Fiber | Sugar |
|---|---|---|---|---|---|---|---|---|
| 337 | 18g | 7g | 15mg | 960mg | 33g | 14g | 4g | 6g |

CARB X-change 2

Total Sodium per serving 391mg

# Stuffed Bacon
# Mushroom Swiss Burgers

## Ingredients:

| | Sodium per serving |
|---|---|
| **20 oz. Lean Ground Beef** | 98mg |
| **2 - 1 oz. Slices of Swiss Cheese**  | 37mg |
| **2 Slices of Low Sodium Bacon** | 48mg |
| **2 Whole Mushrooms,** diced | 0mg |
| **4 Hamburger Buns** | 206mg |

┌─ **fyi:** ────────────────────┐
  I recommend buying a small kitchen
  scale for weighing food.
└──────────────────────────────┘

## How to:

Cook bacon according to package directions, crumble.

Cut swiss cheese and mushrooms into small pieces.

Divide ground beef into 4 equal balls approximately 5 oz. each. Take 1 ball of ground beef and separate out about 1 oz. from each burger.

Pat out remaining beef on a small plate into 4-5" diameter patty on a saucer making a small 2" well in the center of the patty.

Add 1 portion of cheese, mushrooms, and bacon inside the well of each burger.

Pat out the remaining 1 oz. pieces of beef into small patty and place on top of cheese, mushrooms, and bacon.

Fold sides of burger around edges to "seal" the inside of the burger.

Grill until desired doneness.

Yields:  4 servings
(1 serving= 1 - 5 oz. patty with bun)

| Cal | Tot Fat | Sat Fat | Chol. | Potass | Carbs | Prot. | Fiber | Sugar |
|---|---|---|---|---|---|---|---|---|
| 571 | 37g | 15g | 123mg | 766mg | 22g | 35g | 1g | 3g |

Total Sodium per serving
389mg

**94**
**the main dish**

# on the
# side

# Potato Wedges

## Ingredients:

| | Sodium per serving |
|---|---|
| **4 medium potatoes,** scrubbed well | 2mg |
| **3 Tbsp. Canola Oil** | 0mg |
| **1 Tbsp. Fresh Parsley or ½ tbsp. Dried** | <1mg |
| **¼ tsp. Garlic Powder** | 0mg |
| **¼ tsp. Onion Powder** | 0mg |

## How to:

Cut potatoes into wedges where the base is about ½"

In a medium bowl, add remaining ingredients and mix well.

Add potatoes and toss.

Arrange on a baking sheet and bake for 20-25 minutes, turning potatoes once.

Yields: 6 servings (1 serving = Approx. 8 oz.)

| Cal | Tot Fat | Sat Fat | Chol. | Potass | Carbs | Prot. | Fiber | Sugar |
|---|---|---|---|---|---|---|---|---|
| 172 | 7g | <1g | 0mg | 603mg | 25g | 3g | 3g | 1g |

Total Sodium
3mg per serving

# Sour Cream and Onion Mashed Potatoes

**Oven Temp:**
350°F

## Ingredients:

| | Sodium per serving |
|---|---|
| 2 lbs. Potatoes | 14mg |
| ⅓ cup Light Sour Cream  | 11mg |
| ¼ cup Skim Milk | 5mg |
| ¼ cup Green Onion, green part only | <1mg |
| 3 Tbsp. Unsalted Butter | <1mg |
| Pepper to taste | 0mg |

☑ SUPER EASY

## How to:

Peel and slice potatoes into small chunks and place in a large pot.

Cover with water and boil 15-20 minutes or until potatoes are tender.

Drain.

Using electric mixer, mash potatoes and blend in remaining ingredients until creamy.

Yields: 6 servings (1 serving = ½ cup)

| Cal | Tot Fat | Sat Fat | Chol. | Potass | Carbs | Prot. | Fiber | Sugar |
|---|---|---|---|---|---|---|---|---|
| 264 | 7g | 5g | 20mg | 1073mg | 39g | 6g | 6g | 3g |

CARB X-change 2½

Total Sodium per serving
32mg

# Oven Roasted Potatoes

## Ingredients:

| | Sodium per serving |
|---|---|
| 1 lb. Red Potatoes | 7mg |
| 2 Tbsp. Olive Oil | 0mg |
| 1 tsp. Garlic Powder | 0mg |
| ½ tsp. Onion Powder | <1mg |
| ½ tsp. Paprika | 0mg |
| ¼ tsp. Cayenne Pepper (optional) | 0mg |
| ¼ tsp. Black Pepper | 0mg |

## How to:

Wash and cut potatoes into 1" pieces.

Place in a 9" x 13" baking dish.

Pour olive oil over potatoes and toss.

In a small container or jar mix garlic powder, onion powder, paprika, cayenne pepper, and black pepper.

Sprinkle evenly over potatoes.

Place in oven for 30 minutes, turning once half way through.

For crisper potatoes finish off by broiling for 3-4 minutes.

Yields: 4 servings (1 serving = 4 oz.)

| Cal | Tot Fat | Sat Fat | Chol. | Potass | Carbs | Prot. | Fiber | Sugar |
|---|---|---|---|---|---|---|---|---|
| 146 | 7g | 1g | 0mg | 536mg | 19g | 2g | 2g | 1g |

CARB X-change 1

Total Sodium per serving
7mg

# Twice Baked Sweet Potatoes

## Ingredients:

| | Sodium per serving |
|---|---|
| **3 Medium Sweet Potatoes** | 8mg |
| **4 Tbsp. Unsalted Butter** | 2mg |
| **¼ cup Light Brown Sugar**, packed | 4mg |
| **2 oz. Low-Fat Cream Cheese**  | 28mg |
| **¼ tsp. Cinnamon** | 0mg |
| **⅛ tsp. Nutmeg** | 0mg |
| **⅛ tsp. Ginger** | 0mg |
| **1 Cup Mini-Marshmallows** | 6mg |

## How to:

Bake sweet potatoes for about an hour or until done.

In a separate medium bowl, combine remaining ingredients, except marshmallows.

When potatoes are done and cooled, slice lengthwise and scoop flesh out into bowl with mixture in it and reserve skins.

Mix potatoes with a hand blender.

When mixed well, spoon back into skins and place on baking sheet. Top with marshmallows.

Cook for 15 minutes in oven.

Yields: 6 servings (1 serving = 1 skin filled)

## fyi:

**Brown Sugar:** For a healthier recipe, an equivalent brown sugar substitute may be substituted for brown sugar.

| Cal | Tot Fat | Sat Fat | Chol. | Potass | Carbs | Prot. | Fiber | Sugar |
|---|---|---|---|---|---|---|---|---|
| 177 | 9g | 6g | 26mg | 290mg | 21g | 2g | 2g | 12g |

CARB X-change 2

Total Sodium 42mg per serving

# French Fries

## Ingredients:

| | Sodium per serving |
|---|---|
| 2 Large Potatoes | 15mg |
| 1 Tbsp. Olive Oil | 0mg |
| Dust with your favorite No Sodium Seasoning | 0mg |
| (Onion Powder, Garlic Powder, Pepper, Basil, Oregano, Thyme etc.) | |

## How to:

Peel and cut potatoes length-wise, matchstick style.

Pile on cookie sheet and pour olive oil over fries.

Toss to coat.

Spread out on cookie sheet so no sticks are touching each other.

Dust with seasoning or leave plain.

Bake for 20-25 minutes or until golden brown.

For crispy fries, put on top rack and Broil for 3-5 minutes. Watch carefully so they do not burn.

Yields: 4 servings  (1serving = ¼ of fries)

| Cal | Tot Fat | Sat Fat | Chol. | Potass | Carbs | Prot. | Fiber | Sugar |
|---|---|---|---|---|---|---|---|---|
| 169 | 4g | <1g | 0mg | 800mg | 32g | 4g | 3g | 2g |

CARB X-change 2

Total Sodium 15mg per serving

# Garlic Mashed Red Potatoes

## Ingredients:

| Ingredient | Sodium per serving |
|---|---|
| **2 lbs. Red Potatoes,** (cut into small pieces) | 7mg |
| **6 Garlic Cloves** | <1mg |
| **3 Tbsp. Unsalted Butter** | <1mg |
| **¼ cup fresh Parsley,** finely chopped | 1mg |
| **⅓ cup Skim Milk** | 6mg |
| **Pepper to taste** | 0mg |

## How to:

Wash and cut potatoes into ½" chunks.

Peel and smash garlic and add to potatoes.

Place potatoes and garlic in a medium pot, cover with water and cook, covered, on stove for 15-20 minutes or until potatoes are tender.

Drain water and add in remaining ingredients.

Mix with hand mixer until all chunks are gone.

Yields:  8  (1 serving = ½ cup)

| Cal | Tot Fat | Sat Fat | Chol. | Potass | Carbs | Prot. | Fiber | Sugar |
|---|---|---|---|---|---|---|---|---|
| 128 | 5g | 3g | 12mg | 557mg | 19g | 3g | 2g | 1g |

CARB X-change 1

Total Sodium per serving 14mg

# Sweet Potato Fries

## Ingredients:

| | Sodium per serving |
|---|---|
| **2 med. Sweet Potatoes,** (approx. 8 oz. each) | 9mg |
| **2½ Tbsp. Olive Oil** | 0mg |
| **½ tsp. Cinnamon** | 0mg |
| **Pinch of Nutmeg** | 0mg |
| **2 Tbsp. Brown Sugar** | 2mg |

**cooking tip**

**Try to cut fries as even as possible into thin ½ in. sticks to avoid fries being soggy and to cook evenly.**

☑ SUPER EASY

## How to:

In a large bowl, mix olive oil, cinnamon, nutmeg, and brown sugar.

Arrange potatoes on baking sheet so potatoes are not touching each other.

Sprinkle mixture over the top of potatoes.

Bake for 20 minutes, flipping once.

Yields: 4 servings
(1 serving = Approx. 4 oz. of fries)

| Cal | Tot Fat | Sat Fat | Chol. | Potass | Carbs | Prot. | Fiber | Sugar |
|---|---|---|---|---|---|---|---|---|
| 171 | 9g | 1g | 0mg | 159mg | 25g | 1g | 2g | 9g |

CARB X-change 1½

Total Sodium per serving
11mg

# Mashed Sweet Potatoes

| Ingredients: | Sodium per serving |
|---|---|
| 2 lbs. Sweet Potatoes | 10mg |
| 2 Tbsp. Honey | <1mg |
| 2 Tbsp. Unsalted Butter | <1mg |
| ½ tsp. Cinnamon | 0mg |

## How to:

Bake potatoes for 45-60 minutes or until done.

When potatoes are finished, peel skin off and place in a large bowl.

Add remaining ingredients and mix with hand mixer.

Yields: 5 servings (1 serving = Approx. 6 oz. )

☑ SUPER EASY

| Cal | Tot Fat | Sat Fat | Chol. | Potass | Carbs | Prot. | Fiber | Sugar |
|---|---|---|---|---|---|---|---|---|
| 149 | 5g | 3g | 12mg | 166mg | 26g | 1g | 3g | 7g |

CARB X-change 2

Total Sodium per serving 11mg

# Honey Covered
# Sweet Potatoes

**Oven Temp:**
**350°F**

### Ingredients:

| | Sodium per serving |
|---|---|
| **2 lbs. Sweet Potatoes,** (cut into ½" cubes) | 10mg |
| **¼ cup Olive Oil** | 0mg |
| **¼ cup Honey** | <1mg |
| **½ tsp. Cinnamon** | 0mg |

### How to:

Spread out sweet potatoes in a small casserole dish.

In a small bowl, combine remaining ingredients.

Mix well. Pour over sweet potatoes.

Bake for 1 hour, stirring every 15 minutes

Yields:  5 servings  (1 serving = Approx. 6 oz.)

☑SUPER EASY

☑FAMILY FAVORITE

| Cal | Tot Fat | Sat Fat | Chol. | Potass | Carbs | Prot. | Fiber | Sugar |
|---|---|---|---|---|---|---|---|---|
| 230 | 11g | 2g | 0mg | 169mg | 33g | 21g | 3g | 14g |

**CARB** X-change **2**

**Total Sodium** per serving
11mg

# Scalloped Potatoes

## Ingredients:

| | Sodium per serving |
|---|---|
| **1½ lbs. Potatoes,** sliced thin (About 4 medium potatoes) | 1mg |
| **¾ cup Onion,** chopped | <1mg |
| **4 Tbsp. Unsalted Butter,** divided | <1mg |
| **1 tsp. Garlic Powder** | 0mg |
| **2 Tbsp. All-Purpose Flour** | 0mg |
| **¼ tsp. Black Pepper** | 0mg |
| **1¼ cup Skim Milk** | 16mg |
| **1 cup Shredded, Cheddar Cheese** (Optional)  | 70mg |
| **¾ cup Plain Panko Bread Crumbs** | 6mg |
| **Non-Stick Cooking Spray** | |

## How to:

Spray an 8" x 8" (2 quart) dish with non-stick spray.

Layer half of potatoes and half of onions in bottom of dish.

In saucepan, melt 2 Tbsp. unsalted butter; Stir in garlic, flour, and pepper until smooth. Gradually add milk and cheddar cheese.

Heat until sauce thickens. When sauce is done, pour half over potatoes in dish.

Add the other half of potatoes and onions to dish. Top with remaining sauce.

Cover with foil and bake for 45 minutes

(While potatoes are baking) In a small bowl, melt remaining 2 Tbsp. butter, add bread crumbs.

After baking for 45 minutes, take out of oven and top with bread crumbs.

Continue to bake uncovered for 15 more minutes.

Yields: 10 servings (1 serving = ½ cup)

| Cal | Tot Fat | Sat Fat | Chol. | Potass | Carbs | Prot. | Fiber | Sugar |
|---|---|---|---|---|---|---|---|---|
| 190 | 9g | 5g | 25mg | 446mg | 23g | 6g | 2g | 1g |

CARB X-change 1½

Total Sodium 95mg per serving

# Twice Baked Potatoes

## Ingredients:

| | Sodium per serving |
|---|---|
| **4 large Potatoes** | 11mg |
| **1 cup Skim Milk** | 16mg |
| **¾ cup Light Sour Cream**  | 19mg |
| **4 Tbsp. Unsalted Butter,** divided | <1mg |
| **½ tsp. Pepper** | 0mg |
| **1 cup Shredded Cheddar Cheese,** divided | 88mg |
| **8 Green Onions** green part only, chopped and divided | 4mg |
| **4 Slices Low-Sodium Bacon** (optional) | 48mg |

## How to:

Bake potatoes for 1 hr. or until done.
(To speed up prep time, cook potatoes in microwave.)

While potatoes are cooking, cook bacon, crumble, and set aside.

In a large bowl, combine milk, sour cream, butter, pepper, ½ cheese, and ½ green onions.

Mix with hand mixer.

Set in refrigerator until potatoes are done.

When potatoes are done, let cool and slice lengthwise.

Scoop out flesh of potatoes into bowl with sour cream mixture and mix well.

Spoon mixture back into potato skins and top with remaining green onions, chives, and bacon.

Bake for another 15 min.

Yields:  8 servings  (1 serving = ½ potato filled)

---

**fyi:**

**Cheddar Cheese:** Shop and compare the cheeses that your supermarket carries. You may be able to find a low-sodium cheddar. Be aware that a 2% cheddar cheese may contain more sodium than a regular cheddar cheese.

➝Nutritional information is figured with bacon.

| Cal | Tot Fat | Sat Fat | Chol. | Potass | Carbs | Prot. | Fiber | Sugar |
|---|---|---|---|---|---|---|---|---|
| 293 | 13g | 8g | 39mg | 862mg | 36g | 10g | 4g | 3g |

Total Sodium
186mg per serving

# Red Potato Salad

## Ingredients:

| | Sodium per serving |
|---|---|
| **4 lb. Small Red Potatoes,** cut into bite size pieces | 2mg |
| **3 Tbsp. Light Sour Cream** | 3mg |
| **3 Tbsp. Light Mayonnaise** | 15mg |
| **2 Tbsp. Fresh Parsley,** minced | <1mg |
| **1 Green Onion,** green part only, chopped | <1mg |

## How to:

Place potatoes in a medium pan and cover with water.

Place on stove and cook for 20 minutes or until tender.

Drain, and place in a small bowl to let cool.

While waiting for potatoes to cool, combine the remaining ingredients in a small bowl.

Pour mixture over potatoes and mix gently.

Refrigerate for 4 hours before serving.

Yields: 12 servings  (1 serving = ½ oz.)

---

**fyi:**

**Mayonnaise:** I have found the store brand is generally lower in sodium.

---

| Cal | Tot Fat | Sat Fat | Chol. | Potass | Carbs | Prot. | Fiber | Sugar |
|---|---|---|---|---|---|---|---|---|
| 152 | 10g | <1g | 0mg | 378mg | 12g | 4g | 4g | <1g |

CARB X-change ½

Total Sodium per serving 42mg

# Grilled Corn on the Cob

## Ingredients:

| | Sodium per serving |
|---|---|
| **4 Ears of Corn** (Husks removed and corn cleaned) | 22mg |
| **5 Tbsp. Unsalted Butter** | 2mg |
| **2 Tbsp. Garlic**, minced | <1mg |
| **1 Tbsp. Fresh Parsley or ½ Tbsp. Dried Parsley** | <1mg |

## How to:

Melt unsalted butter in a small bowl and add garlic and parsley.

Place corn on grill and baste with garlic butter.

Continue grilling on medium heat, turning and basting every couple of minutes until corn starts to brown.

Yields: 4 servings (1 serving = 1 ear of corn)

| Cal | Tot Fat | Sat Fat | Chol. | Potass | Carbs | Prot. | Fiber | Sugar |
|---|---|---|---|---|---|---|---|---|
| 183 | 13g | 7g | 31mg | 261mg | 18g | 3g | 3g | 3g |

CARB X-change 1

Total Sodium 24mg per serving

# Baked Asparagus

**Oven Temp:**
450°F

### Ingredients:

| | Sodium per serving |
|---|---|
| **1 lb. Asparagus,** trimmed | 2mg |
| **2 tsp. Olive Oil** | 0mg |
| **1 Tbsp. Parmesan Cheese,** grated | 21mg |
| **½ cup Plain Panko Bread Crumbs** | 10mg |
| **Non-Stick Cooking Spray** | |

### How to:

Spray a 9" x 13" dish with non-stick spray.

Spread asparagus out in dish.

Pour olive oil over asparagus and toss gently.

Sprinkle parmesan and bread crumbs over asparagus.

Bake for 20 minutes.

Yields:  4 servings  (1 serving = 4 oz. asparagus)

☑ SUPER EASY

| Cal | Tot Fat | Sat Fat | Chol. | Potass | Carbs | Prot. | Fiber | Sugar |
|---|---|---|---|---|---|---|---|---|
| 70 | 3g | <1g | 1mg | 205mg | 10g | 3g | 2g | <1g |

CARB X-change ½

Total Sodium per serving
33mg

# Cucumber and Onion

## Ingredients:

| | Sodium per serving |
|---|---|
| 1 large Cucumber | 1mg |
| 1 small Vidalia Onion | <1mg |
| ½ cup White Vinegar | 0mg |
| ⅓ cup of Sugar | 0mg |
| 2 Tbsp. Water | 0mg |
| ½ tsp. Celery Seed | <1mg |

## fyi:

**Sugar:** For a healthier recipe, an equivalent sugar substitute may be substituted for sugar.

☑ SUPER EASY

## How to:

Slice cucumber and onion to ⅛" to ¼".

In a medium bowl, mix vinegar, sugar, water, and celery seed.

Add cucumber and onion and let set in refrigerator overnight.

Yields: 6 servings (1 serving = Approx. ½ cup)

| Cal | Tot Fat | Sat Fat | Chol. | Potass | Carbs | Prot. | Fiber | Sugar |
|---|---|---|---|---|---|---|---|---|
| 54 | <1g | 0g | 0mg | 93mg | 14g | <1g | <1g | 11g |

CARB X-change 1

Total Sodium per serving 2mg

# Asparagus with Sesame Oil Dressing

## Ingredients:

|  | Sodium per serving |
|---|---|
| **2 lbs. Asparagus** (about 15-20 stalks), trimmed | 10mg |
| **2 Garlic Cloves,** minced | 0mg |
| **½ tsp. Black Pepper** | 0mg |
| **2 tsp. Dijon Mustard** | 14mg |
| **1½ Tbsp. Lemon Juice** | 0mg |
| **¼ cup Sesame Oil** | 0mg |
| **1 Tbsp. Sesame Seeds** | 0mg |

## How to:

Bring a medium sauce pan of water to a boil.

Cook asparagus 3-6 minutes depending on thickness.

When done, rinse in cool water.

In a medium bowl whisk together garlic, pepper, mustard, lemon juice, and sesame oil.

Pour over asparagus and toss.

Top with sesame seeds.

Place in oven for 15 minutes.

Yields:  4 servings  (1 serving = 8 oz. asparagus)

| Cal | Tot Fat | Sat Fat | Chol. | Potass | Carbs | Prot. | Fiber | Sugar |
|---|---|---|---|---|---|---|---|---|
| 172 | 15g | 2g | 0mg | 300mg | 6g | 3g | 3g | <1g |

CARB
X-change ½

Total Sodium
per serving
24mg

# Tropical 5 Cup Salad

## Ingredients:

| | Sodium per serving |
|---|---|
| 2 cups Miniature Marshmallows | 7mg |
| ¾ cup Flaked Coconut | 2mg |
| 1-(11 oz.) can of Mandarin Oranges, drained | 2mg |
| 1- (8 oz.) can of Crushed Pineapple, drained | <1mg |
| ¾ cup Light Sour Cream | 19mg |
| ½ Tbsp. Maraschino Cherry Juice | <1mg |

## How to:

Mix all ingredients well in a medium bowl.

Serve chilled.

Yields: 8 servings (1 serving = Approx. ½ cup)

| Cal | Tot Fat | Sat Fat | Chol. | Potass | Carbs | Prot. | Fiber | Sugar |
|---|---|---|---|---|---|---|---|---|
| 150 | 4g | 4g | 8mg | 84mg | 26g | 2g | <1g | 22g |

CARB X-change **2**

Total Sodium per serving 31mg

# Cole Slaw

## Ingredients:

| | Sodium per serving |
|---|---|
| ½ cup Light Mayonnaise 🛒 | 48mg |
| ⅓ cup Sugar | 0mg |
| ½ cup Skim Milk | 6mg |
| 2½ Tbsp. Lemon Juice | 0mg |
| 2½ Tbsp. White Vinegar | 0mg |
| ⅛ tsp. Black Pepper | 0mg |
| 1 tsp. Poppy Seeds | 0mg |
| 24 oz. (by weight) **Cabbage,** finely shredded, (about 5 cups) | 10mg |
| ½ cup **Carrot,** shredded | 4mg |
| 3 Tbsp. **Onion,** minced | <1mg |

### fyi:

**Sugar:** For a healthier recipe, an equivalent sugar substitute may be substituted for sugar.

**Mayonnaise:** I have found the store brand is generally lower in sodium.

☑ FAMILY FAVORITE

## How to:

Mix all ingredients except cabbage, carrot, and onion.

In a different bowl, combine cabbage, carrot and onion.

Pour liquid over cabbage mix and let set overnight.

The longer the slaw marinates the better the flavor!

Yields: 10 servings (1 serving = ½ cup)

| Cal | Tot Fat | Sat Fat | Chol. | Potass | Carbs | Prot. | Fiber | Sugar |
|---|---|---|---|---|---|---|---|---|
| 78 | 3g | <1g | <1mg | 189mg | 12g | 1g | 2g | 7g |

CARB X-change 1

Total Sodium per serving 69mg

# Baked Beans

## Ingredients:

| Ingredient | Sodium per serving |
|---|---|
| 2 - 14.5 oz. can of Pinto Beans 🛒 | 75mg |
| 1 Tbsp. Corn Starch | 0mg |
| ½ cup NSA Ketchup | 0mg |
| ⅓ cup White Wine Vinegar | 0mg |
| ⅓ cup Brown Sugar, packed | |
| ⅓ cup Onion, chopped | <1mg |
| 3 Tbsp. Barbeque Sauce 🛒 | 11mg |
| The Memphis BBQ Sauce is a great choice. (see recipe page 25) | |
| 1 tsp. Yellow Mustard | 14mg |
| ½ tsp. Hickory Liquid Smoke | 0mg |
| ½ tsp. Chili Powder | 5mg |
| ¼ tsp. Black Pepper | 0mg |
| ¼ tsp. Garlic Powder | 0mg |

## How to:

Pour beans in 8" x 8" casserole dish.

In a small bowl, combine remaining ingredients and pour over beans.

Cover and place in oven.

Bake for 90 minutes stirring 2-3 times.

Yields: 8 servings (1 serving = ½ cup)

---

## fyi:

**Beans:** Draining and rinsing your beans throroughly will dramatically decrease the sodium content.

**Chili Powder:** A no sodium chili powder is available in specialty stores or see recipe on page 5.

**Brown Sugar:** For a healthier recipe, an equivalent brown sugar substitute may be substituted for brown sugar.

☑ FAMILY FAVORITE

| Cal | Tot Fat | Sat Fat | Chol. | Potass | Carbs | Prot. | Fiber | Sugar |
|---|---|---|---|---|---|---|---|---|
| 142 | <1g | 0g | 0mg | 235mg | 28g | 4g | 10g | 17g |

CARB X-change 2

Total Sodium per serving
107mg

# Sweet Carrots

## Ingredients:

| | Sodium per serving |
|---|---|
| **1 lb. Carrots,** (about 4 large) cut into small pieces | 22mg |
| **4 Tbsp. Unsalted Butter** | <1mg |
| **5 Tbsp. Light Brown Sugar**, packed | 0mg |
| **¼ tsp. Cinnamon** | 0mg |
| **1 Large Microwave Steam Bag** | |

## How to:

Combine all ingredients in steam bag and cook to bag's specifications.

Yields: 8 servings (1 serving = Approx. ⅓ cup)

## fyi:

**Brown Sugar:** For a healthier recipe, an equivalent brown sugar substitute may be substituted for brown sugar.

☑SUPER EASY

| Cal | Tot Fat | Sat Fat | Chol. | Potass | Carbs | Prot. | Fiber | Sugar |
|---|---|---|---|---|---|---|---|---|
| 98 | 6g | 4g | 15mg | 147mg | 15g | <12g | 1g | 13g |

CARB X-change 1

Total Sodium 23mg per serving

# Pasta Salad

Just Mix
Recipe

## Ingredients:

| | Sodium per serving |
|---|---|
| 1 - 16 oz. Box of Tri-Color Pasta | 0mg |
| 3 cups of your favorite Vegetables, (bite size pieces) | 0mg |

**Dressing:**

| | |
|---|---|
| 2 Tbsp. Italian Dressing Mix (See recipe on page 6.) | 0mg |
| ½ cup White Wine Vinegar | 0mg |
| ⅓ Water | 0mg |
| ⅓ cup Canola Oil | 0mg |
| 1½ tsp. Fresh Lemon Juice | <1mg |
| 1 Tbsp. Light Corn Syrup | 2mg |
| 2 Tbsp. Parmesan Cheese | 17mg |

## How to:

Cook pasta for 8-9 minutes or until tender.

Drain and set aside.

Cut vegetables into bite size pieces and combine with pasta in a large bowl.

In a small food processor or small bowl, combine dressing and combine with pasta.

Yields: 10 servings (1 serving = Approx. ½ cup)

| Cal | Tot Fat | Sat Fat | Chol. | Potass | Carbs | Prot. | Fiber | Sugar |
|---|---|---|---|---|---|---|---|---|
| 176 | <1g | 0g | 0mg | 46mg | 37g | 6g | 2g | 3g |

Total Sodium per serving
7mg

# The Easiest Green Beans

## Ingredients:

| | Sodium per serving |
|---|---|
| **1 lb. Fresh Green Beans** | 3mg |
| **2 Garlic Cloves,** minced | <1mg |
| **2 Slices of Low Sodium Bacon** | 32mg |
| **⅓ cup Onion,** chopped | <1mg |
| **¼ cup Water** | 0mg |
| **½ tsp. Basil** | 0mg |
| **Black Pepper to taste** | 0mg |

## How to:

Cut ends of green beans and place in a medium pan and add remaining ingredients.

Simmer on low heat for 25-30 minutes.

Yields: 6 servings  (1 serving = ½ cup)

☑ SUPER EASY

| Cal | Tot Fat | Sat Fat | Chol. | Potass | Carbs | Prot. | Fiber | Sugar |
|---|---|---|---|---|---|---|---|---|
| 36 | 1g | 1g | 3mg | 135mg | 5g | 2g | 2g | 0g |

CARB X-change 0

Total Sodium 36mg per serving

# Roasted Broccoli

**Oven Temp:**
425°F

## Ingredients:

| | Sodium per serving |
|---|---|
| **1 lb. Broccoli,** cut into bite size pieces | 16mg |
| **3 Tbsp. Olive Oil** | 0mg |
| **3 Garlic Cloves,** minced | 0mg |
| **1 tsp. Salt-Free Lemon Pepper Seasoning** | 0mg |
| **½ cup Plain Panko Bread Crumbs** | 5mg |

## How to:

Place cut broccoli in large bowl and add olive oil, garlic, lemon pepper, and mix well.

Add Panko and mix again.

Place broccoli in large casserole dish or cake pan and bake in oven for 15-20 minutes or until broccoli cooks to desired tenderness.

Yields: 4 servings  (1 serving = 4 oz.)

☑ SUPER EASY

| Cal | Tot Fat | Sat Fat | Chol. | Potass | Carbs | Prot. | Fiber | Sugar |
|---|---|---|---|---|---|---|---|---|
| 152 | 10g | <1g | 0mg | 378mg | 12g | 4g | 4g | <1g |

**CARB** X-change ½

**Total Sodium** 42mg per serving

# Notes:

# Notes:

# Notes:

# Notes: